BODY-LINE?

HAROLD LARWOOD

ETT IMPRINT
Exile Bay

New edition published by ETT Imprint, Exile Bay 2020

First published by Elkin Matthews, London 1933
First electronic edition published by ETT Imprint, Exile Bay 2017

Copyright © Estate of Harold Larwood 2017, 2020

This book is copyright.

Apart from any fair dealing for the purposes of private study, research, criticism or review, as permitted under the Copyright Act, no part may be reproduced by any process without written permission. Inquiries should be addressed to the publishers, on ettimprint@hotmail.com or by mail to:

ETT IMPRINT
PO Box R1906
Royal Exchange NSW 1225
Australia

ISBN 978-1-922384-00-4 (pback)

ISBN 978-1-925706-32-1 (ebook)

All internal photographs courtesy of Iain and Enid Todd, with many from the author's own albums, that were not in the original published edition

Cover and internal design by Tom Thompson

A FOREWORD BY D. R. JARDINE

May 8th 1933.

My dear Harold

You ask me to write a short foreword to your book.
I am glad & proud to try to do so.
Perhaps this as an open letter will meet the case?
Let me begin by wishing you good luck as an author, &
wishing your book a bumper sale.

The Team read of your triumphant reception on your return
to Nottingham with a thrill. It was no more than you
deserved.

It is curious to think that had you been playing for Australia
you would have been the most popular man in Australia!
As it is, I gather that you were not even permitted to depart
unmolested & in peace.

No bowler I venture to say has ever had to contend with more
than, well to you "it", or "stuck it" more magnificently —
& by the same token, no bowler can show a fairer, finer
or more convincing record.

More than half the thirty three wickets you took in the
Test Matches were clean bowled, or it's equivalent
leg before wicket — eighteen to be exact.

This on the perfect toned down wickets of Australia, where numbers one to seven in the batting orders are far less frequently clean bowled than in England. If this isn't bowling at the wicket I don't know what is – as Mr. M. Noble the old Australian Captain wrote of you when summing up the Tour –

"It is all humbug to say that his tactics were unfair, or that he bowled at the man instead of the wicket. He didn't. I could see no difference in his methods from those he used during his previous visit."

Have you heard the sound film of the Third Test Match? I am told that it is louder than a war film, & has been a revelation to folks at home!

We were all hoping that you might break the record for the number of wickets taken in a Test series – but this was not to be, but only missed at that in the last Test & the injury to your foot prevented it.

Your great innings in that match was some compensation – how I wish you'd got those extra two runs.

Good luck Harold, from a very grateful & admiring "Skipper"

Yours ever

DR Jardine

AUTHOR'S PREFACE

I should like to state at the beginning of my book that what is stated in it on controversial matters is my own firm opinion, except where in a few cases the views of other people are published and their names given.

I wish to make it clear that though there were, and are, sharp differences of opinion on the subject of Fast-Leg-Theory bowling between myself and some Australians, there was always an atmosphere of complete cordiality between the teams on both sides. Although we differ seriously over my Fast-Leg-Theory bowling I have done my best in the following pages not to disturb that atmosphere.

Until now my side of the matter has not been heard. I have refused many tempting offers to break silence. As a fast bowler and a hitter by nature I have written strongly because I cannot express myself otherwise.

I hope very much indeed that in doing so, though I was one, of the aggrieved parties in Australia, I have given nobody half the offence from which I suffered so often on the last tour.

A belief exists that some of the things I have written about are not yet to be discussed.

Obviously I differ from that view. I do so because I feel that in a matter of such vital interest to cricketers as the possible admission by legislation of such a far-reaching principle as that bowlers may not bowl as they like, no cricketer can keep silent. I believe I have only written here what very many cricketers are saying. But I have written supported by first-hand knowledge.

For the many imperfections of style and language in my first book I beg the indulgence of my reader.

Yours sincerely
H. Larwood

Jardine directing his players, 1st Test at the Sydney Cricket Ground.
England's Cricket Team for the 3rd Test, Adelaide. Back row: George Duckworth, Tommy Mitchell, Nawab of Pataudi, Maurice Leyland, Harold Larwood, Eddie Paynter, W. Ferguson (scorer). Middle row: Pelham Warner (co-manager), Les Ames, Hedley Verity, Bill Voce, Bill Bowes, Freddie Brown, Maurice Tate, R. C. N. Palairet (co-manager). Front row: Herbert Sutcliffe, Bob Wyatt, Douglas Jardine, Gubby Allen, Wally Hammond

CONTENTS

I. FAST-LEG-THEORY – Fast-Leg-Theory – Its Birth, its Development in Australia, its Fairness and its Future.   9

II. THE AUSTRALIAN DOCTORS' REMEDY – Thank Goodness Cricket's Laws are made by M.C.C. – A Thoroughly Impracticable Proposal – Are Umpires Thought-Readers? – The Legal Side of the Matter – Will Umpires Accept the Responsibility? – My Remedy, if there is one.   26

III. MY VIEWS ON BARRACKING – A Noisy Majority – Can Past Australian Test Players Do Nothing? – Drivel on the Stage – Threatening Letters – I Don't Look Like a Murderer! – A Friend in Benalla – The Quorn Incident – A Half-Chewed Farewell.   37

IV. IN RE BRADMAN v. LARWOOD – Don finds the "Easy-looking Pie" to be Mostly Crust.   50

V. THE FIRST TEST – Our Disappointment at Bradman's Absence – A Good Sydney Wicket and a Good Start – Fast-Leg-Theory used Intensively for the First Time in Test Cricket – McCabe's Splendid Innings – My Ten Wickets.   60

VI. THE SECOND TEST – That Wicket – The Truth about it – O'Reilly takes his Place among Test Rank Bowlers – Oh! for a Pair of Boots.   68

VII. THE THIRD TEST – The "Atmosphere" Match. – Six Days' Tension – An Attack of Hysteria – Batsmen Unluckily Hit – Splendid Batting by Leyland Paynter and Mr. Wyatt – Did Ironmonger use Resin, or Eucalyptus Oil? – Fast Bowling again Beats Australia.   74

VIII. THE FOURTH TEST – The Ashes Regained – England Wins at the last place on Earth fit for Test Cricket in February – Lancashire and Yorkshire much to the Fore – Paynter's Ward-to-Wicket Cricket.   84

IX. THE FIFTH TEST – We Drop some Difficult Catches – Don tries to Hit me to the Off – Awkward Facts for Australia's Board of Control! – Alexander's Footmarks – Mr. Wyatt again Bats Well – Hammond's Big Hit – He Ends a Fiery Rubber with a Crashing Six!   92

X. AUSTRALIA NOW – AND TO-MORROW   105

XI. THE FAST BOWLER'S JOB   111

XII. MY HOME AT TRENT BRIDGE – Introduced by Joe Hardstaff – A few Wrinkles for Young Professionals – A Great Trio, Mr. Arthur Carr, Jimmy Iremonger and George Gunn – My Seven Seasons' Bag of Wickets – Some Star Batsmen – The Last Over.   120

Appendix   133

CHAPTER 1

Fast-Leg-Theory

FAST-LEG-THEORY – ITS BIRTH, ITS DEVELOPMENT IN AUSTRALIA, ITS FAIRNESS, AND ITS FUTURE.

FAST-LEG-THEORY bowling was born in the Test match at Kennington Oval in August, 1930, unknown to anybody but myself.

A spot of rain had fallen. The ball was "popping." My great friend the late Archie Jackson stood up to me, getting pinked once or twice in the process, and he never flinched. With Bradman it was different. It was because of that difference that I determined, then and there, that if I was again honoured with an invitation to go to Australia I would not forget that difference.

I am aware that it is claimed that Gregory and Macdonald bowled it in 1919 and 1921, but neither of them bowled true Fast-LegTheory. Neither had my setting of the legside field, and without that there can be no genuine Fast-Leg-Theory. Everything else is only a kind of imitation.

I was soon convinced that, to be really effective, Fast-Leg-Theory must have accuracy with pace as its *very first* essentials. Without accuracy on the part of the bowler it might be a very dangerous thing for the batsman. I claim to have acquired that Accuracy.

During the last two Seasons in England I made of Accuracy something more than a study. "Accuracy or nothing" became my watchword. Whether I succeeded or not I must let my readers judge by giving here for purposes of comparison my figures for the past three seasons in English cricket.

Remember, the 1930 figures were achieved before I had studied Leg-Theory, and before I had had a dental operation after the season of 1930, which effected a vast improvement in my general health and strength. The word "Place" denotes where I finished in the Season's averages.

	Place	Overs	Maidens	Runs	Wickets	Average
1930	. 4th	621	124	1622	99	16·38
1931	. 1st	651	142	1553	129	12·03
1932	. 1st	866	203	2084	162	12·86

I think I am justified in laying stress on the facts that I have bowled an increased number of overs each year, with an increase in the total of wickets taken; an increase in the number of overs not scored off; and a marked decrease in the number of runs scored per wicket obtained.

By way of evidence that I am justified in laying claim to having acquired accuracy since 1930 I hope I may refer here to two facts about my bowling which I believe any interested statistician will confirm.

One is that, speaking generally, my bowling is seldom "pasted."

Another that in the runs scored off me hit fours are in a conspicuous minority. Most fours off me are snicked ones. I have been hit for six only three times in first-class cricket.

I give now my Test match figures for 1928 to 1933. I hope I may be pardoned for stating that throughout 1930 my health was not good. It was in that year I broke down during the first Test, and retired from it.

	Place	Overs	Mds.	Runs	Wkts.	Avge.
In Australia *1928-29	3rd	258.7	41	728	18	40.4
In England 1930	—	101	18	292	4	73.00
In Australia 1932-33	1st	220.2	41	641	33	19.51

* On this tour the 8-ball over was in vogue. That entailed a tremendous strain on a bowler like myself who delivers off the 14th step. Ses my Chapter on The Fast Bowler's Job.

My study of the need for accuracy has, I consider, borne fruit. Without it such results as I have been lucky enough to get could not have been recorded.

The acquisition of this accuracy enables me to bowl at the pace I do without injury to the batsman opposed to me, since I can assure my readers that whether they believe it or not it would be possible for me, *if the intention was there,* which I can assure the world of cricket it never has been, to make it very much more uncomfortable for the majority of batsmen than I do.

There are batsmen I could hit about twice an over if I wished to. I had better, perhaps, not name these!

I give here the origin of the term "Body Line."

It was maliciously coined by a cute Australian journalist for the express purpose of misleading, and for obscuring the issue, which it did with great success. The mere use of the word "Body" was meant to damn me, and damn me it did. Quite as successfully as did any of the batsmen who had to cope with it. The term being brief was very suitable for a sort of war-cry, and that it became.

But I should like to know whether those little thinkers who prefer to call my bowling Body-Line bowling do not see something very significant in the facts that, if it is really what that term implies, none of the less accomplished batsmen among the Australian players was ever hit; the only player who was hit on the head being Bill Oldfield, who said to me himself, the moment after the blow, that it was not my fault; while the only one at all severely struck on the body was that essentially firmfooted and almost immobile player W. M. Woodfull?

Yet, I bowled 220 overs, 1,320 balls, in the Tests, and 296.1 overs, or 1,777 balls altogether, on the whole tour.

If my bowling is Body-Line, if the accusation levelled at me over and over again in Australia is true that I bowled *at* the body, then either I must be extraordinarily inaccurate, or Australian batsmen must be exceptionally clever at avoiding a very fast-moving ball.

The cricket fact of this matter is that bowling of my pace on fast hard wickets if aimed at the batsman, that is to say *if it really was Body-Line bowling*, would be really dangerous to the batsman.

Inasmuch as throughout the last tour in Australia-which I must remind my readers has been the only real test on hard wickets of Fast-Leg-Theory in cricket's history-only two batsmen were at all severely struck by the ball, one of them, by his own frank admission, owing to his own fault, I hold that it is finally proved that

(i) my Leg-Theory bowling is *not* Body-Line bowling.

(ii) my Leg-Theory bowling is not more physically dangerous to the batsman than is any very fast bowling.

(iii) actually it is *much* less physically dangerous than is very fast bowling for which the bowler has not set the leg-side field which warns the batsman what to expect.

I have no excuses to make for bowling which I shall always hold needs no excuse.

My conscience is absolutely clear that I have never bowled at any batsman, and I know that I never shall. I am afraid that any who do not take my word for this must make the best they can of doing the other thing.

But I should like to ask them one thing:

"If I am not speaking the truth why did the M.C.C. honour me by inviting me to go to Australia after their selectors knew my form to the last ounce; and why did Mr. Jardine, put me *on*, and keep me *on*, if I was the least bit likely to bowl other than quite fairly?"

I must here give in full the very interesting article which the former Australian cricketer, J. W. Trumble, contributed to the Melbourne *Argus* of January 23, 1933. From this perfectly spontaneous expression of opinion it is obvious that not every one in Australia agrees either with those who squealed about Body-Line, or with the Australian Board of Control.

Here is the article verbatim:-

THE LEG-THEORY ATTACK

Why it is Justifiable

By J. W. TRUMBLE

The leg-theory attack, rather ungenerously called "body bowling," adopted by the English team in its important matches of the present tour has occasioned more stir in the cricket world than anything else that has happened in the history of the game. Feeling has been running so high and condemnation of the attack has been so bitter that it is difficult now to procure a calm consideration of the matter in all its aspects. I refrained from writing on the subject while the protest of the Board of Control was before the committee of the Marylebone Cricket Club for consideration, but I feel I am now at liberty to do so.

I disagree with the popular view of the leg theory attack. I consider it quite legitimate and justifiable in Test cricket. It is absurd to suggest that the fast bowler in on-side bowling is deliberately bowling at the batsman with the intention of hitting him. No such thing, I am sure, ever enters the bowler's mind. Leg-theory bowling is not dangerous to the batsman unless the condition of the wicket makes it so, and batsmen who can play fast bowling are well able to deal with on-side fast bowling. *There are, however, batsmen who cannot play on-side fast bowling and who do not like it.* It is mainly because of this that objection to the leg-theory attack has been offered. This form of attack is not new, as we have been given to understand. It has been practised at times for some years, and apparently even by our Australian fast bowler Macdonald. It is reported of him in the *Cricketer* of June 18, 1927, that in the match Lancashire *v.* Yorkshire he adopted the leg-theory attack, and bowled with no slips and four leg traps, but without success.

As I see it, the trouble really is Larwood's high-class bowling on wickets favourable to him for results. He is a far better bowler on our wickets than he was four years ago. His delivery is unquestionably fair, and for a bowler of his pace he has wonderful accuracy and length. The facing of his bowling on our concrete-conditioned wickets is, I admit, something of an ordeal, but batsmen have on occasion to face awkward conditions. In early days batsmen had to face worse situations at times. I remember once having to bat on the M.C.C. ground against Turner and Ferris on a pig of a wicket – much worse than any sticky wicket of the present time. In the first innings I was bowled by Turner without scoring, though I thought I had the wicket well covered up with my pads. In the second innings, though the wicket was no better, I managed to withstand the attack, but only at heavy cost. *I was hit about 20 times all over the body by quick-rising balls. I had also the difficulty to contend with, as in the leg-theory attack, of steering clear of the close in-field waiting for catches. We must take the rough with the smooth; it is all in the game.*

A VILLAGE GREEN DECISION

This reminds me of an amusing cricket story oi which I was told when lately in England. The scene was set in a little village in the country far removed from the stir of city life. The occasion was the annual match between two neighbouring villages, as important to them almost as a Test match is to us. The visiting side was batting, and for the home side its "star" bowler, the village blacksmith, a bumpy, fast bowler of the worst type, was striking terror into the hearts of the opposing batsmen on the uncertain pitch. As the game progressed a timid-looking little fellow had to come in and face the ordeal. He bravely stood his ground and survived l-b-w appeals for balls hitting him in various parts of the body. Ultimately a ball hit him in the stomach, which brought him to the ground. While he was there, unconcerned as to outside matters, the umpire, in answer to the bowler's frantic appeal, gave the following decision: – "If the little gentleman has had enough he's out; if not he can go on."

It has been repeatedly suggested by the critics of the English bowling that the old-time fast bowlers did not bowl short-length bowling. I agree that they did not, as a rule, bowl short stuff, more especially on the old-time turf wickets, not because it was not sporting, but because, as it did not rise, short-pitched bowling in those days was looked upon as rubbish, and generally had heavy punishment, particularly from batsmen of the forcing type. *On turf wickets fast bowling did not pay, as a rule, mainly because it did not rise, and it was simple to play.* Spofforth gave it up. I believe that Blackham, if given a sound turf wicket, would have stood up at the wicket to bowling of the class of the present English fast bowling, but he could not do this on our present-day, concrete-conditioned wickets. He stood at the wickets to Spofforth, and to all the Australian bowlers of his time.

Kortright, the Essex amateur,· was, in my opinion, the fastest of all the fast bowlers I have seen. I saw him in action for the M.C.C. against the Australians at Lord's in 1893, and I have an amused recollection of one of his successes in this match. A. H. Jarvis, a great wicket-keeper and a sound bat, was a member of the 1893 Australian Eleven. He played in the match. Jarvis, on going in to bat, had to face Kortright. The first and only ball he received was a yorker of terrific pace, which sent the stumps flying, with Jarvis's bat hardly started on the way down. In the second innings Jarvis had to face the same situation. I was sitting on a form with Spofforth, alongside the passage-way from the pavilion to the wicket. As Jarvis passed us Spofforth said, to the amusement of those around, "Jarvey, old man, start this time where you knocked off last or he will have you again." It was no good. Jarvis did his best, but another high-speed yorker, for which he was late again, sent his stumps flying. Kortright's bowling in this match did not rise anything like it would here, and the batsmen were in no difficulty in facing it wherever it pitched. (See Chapter 10. H.L.)

In my last match in first-class cricket I played in 1893 with Murdoch and Ferris for C. I. Thornton's Gentlemen of England team, with Mold, against Cambridge. Mold was a professional, and the leading fast bowler of the time. The Cambridge team included "Ranji" and F. S. Jackson. It was a strong side. Mold bowled a lot in the match, but with only moderate success. The wicket was a good turf wicket, and I never saw Mold at any time rise to any extent over the stumps. When on tour in England in 1886 we did not meet a fast bowler of any class in any of the county matches. Fast bowlers were then very little in the game, because very few of them were good enough. The great bowlers of the day were all medium-pace, spin bowlers. Lockwood, the famous Surrey express, appeared first against us in 1886 as a colt in the Nottingham team in our match against Nottingham. I happened to go in first. I had to take strike to Lockwood, who, as I took guard, was near the bowling crease, and began to bowl from a position about three yards back. I took him to be a slow bowler, but got the surprise of my life. The ball came along like a flash, and only that it rose a bit and hit me on the elbow it would have been clean through to the stumps. I was satisfied after this that there was no occasion for a fast bowler to take a run of 15 to 20 yards to get up pace. Lockwood later took on a longer run.

WHEN BOWLING IS OBJECTIONABLE

If the wicket is as it should be there is not much danger in fast bowling, whether it be on-side or otherwise. In my view high rising bowling, whether on the stumps or on the off, where batsmen mostly leave it alone, is just as objectionable as high rising bowling on the on-side of the wicket. All of it is destructive of good batting. We never see now the good cutting off-side play and out-field hitting we had in cricket on the old-time turf wicket. The hard clay condition of present-day wickets is responsible for the high-rising ball coming from fast bowling. Were it not for this I think the leg theory would be rarely practised. At a Test match in Sydney some years ago during a period of deadly slow play, Bill Howell caused amusement by calling out to my brother, "I say, Hughie, what's this new rule in the game? I'm told that if you hit a ball over the bowler's head you are out and if you hit it out of the ground they won't let you play any more?" Old Bill was one of the hefty hitters of his time, and the slow play he was witnessing had him "fed up."

We are in the wrong in the attitude we have taken up toward the leg-theory attack. I know I am in conflict with the views of many other international cricketers, but the knowledge I obtained while resident in the Wimmera, in close touch with the Department of Agriculture, of soils, their composition, and their effect in operation, added to my experience of first-class cricket, more particularly of play on genuine turf wickets, has enabled me to examine and consider the position from all sides. *I would be interested to see our team adopt the leg-theory attack against the present English team, not by way of reprisal, but to see how batsmen more accustomed to this form of attack play it.*

Last Saturday I advocated a reform of the wicket. A further reform required is a reform of the constitution of the Board now controlling the game. Recent events have disclosed a serious weakness in personnel. The M.C.C. committee controlling the game in England is guided mainly by men on the committee having international cricket experience. It is not so with us. A strong Board of Control is needed now more than ever. We can never have a Board giving complete public confidence which is devoid of representatives having experience of international cricket. At least one of the representatives from each State should be a cricketer having such experience. The two States which have only one representative on the Board might be exempted from this provision.

* * * *

I have taken the liberty of italicising certain passages which I consider help to prove my case.

Concerning the future of Fast-Leg-Theory much might be written. Here I am rather tied down. I am like a father defending his offspring, though I am not really the fond parent whose child can do no wrong.

In Fast-Leg-Theory, fairly utilised, there is no wrong.

And, taking all the circumstances into consideration, the distance the bowler is from the batsman, the weight of the ball, and the probably highest momentum a bowler can impart to a missile of that weight, I can see a very small margin for unfair bowling.

With the politics of the game I have no concern. Indeed, they are no concern of mine. My only job in life is to get as many wickets as I can for

Notts., for the Players, and for England.

Deeds not words are what interest me most.

Therefore, I am naturally jealous of that particular branch of the game of cricket which I invented, and at which I claim to have arrived at a sufficient state of perfection to earn at least the respect of my opponents.

So it is my resolute determination that if anything is done with the purpose of preventing, or which in practice will have the effect of diminishing my destructiveness as a bowler of Fast-Leg-Theory then, to use an American term, I quit.

I shall retire from first-class county cricket as soon as my contract permits immediately after either Fast-Leg-Theory is stopped, or county captains agree by a majority vote, or otherwise, not to use it.

In this matter I listen on the field only to the orders of my captain. If his hands are manacled so far as Leg-Theory is concerned, from that moment I shall realise that the knell of my career in first-class cricket is rung.

The loss will be mine, for I love this game and no man has ever loved it more. I live for cricket. I have always tried my hardest to keep physically fit to do my very utmost for my side and my club, and I should not quit the arena without the deepest pang of regret. But, having found, and to the best of my ability perfected, a perfectly fair way to get wickets, if I· was then deprived of the right to utilise my art, such as it is, I should be false and unfair to myself if I agreed to remain in the game.

I have discussed the whole matter with brother professionals, and I cannot find one who thinks that Leg-Theory *can* be stopped by legislation.

Any such legislation would govern the play of all cricketers. There cannot be an enactment affecting fast bowlers only. If, therefore, for example, in an effort to end Leg-Theory, the number of fielders on the leg-side was limited, or the number allowed to be posted within a fixed distance of the batsman on the leg-side was to be limited, what would become of the medium and slow-medium off-break bowlers on a sticky wicket? Their livelihood, on the rare occasions when they can justly hope to reap a fair harvest of wickets, would be greatly diminished, if it did not disappear.

Take the case of bowlers like George Geary and Sam Staples on a rain and sun damaged pitch. What becomes of their chance if they are not allowed to have three short-legs within a dozen yards of the bat? Other instances would not be difficult to find.

I am aware that there is a fairly general impression that Fast-Leg-Theory if widely indulged in would render the game monotonous and dull for the onlookers. Why this should follow as a matter of course I cannot see. In case mine is regarded as a prejudiced opinion let me cite three specific instances of interesting cricket in the face of Fast-Leg-Theory. This was extensively used by myself and Bill Voce last season against Glamorgan at Cardiff. We had scored 386 but our opponents put that completely in the shade by making 502, and it is possible that had they held catches in our second innings we should have been beaten. In spite of Fast-Leg-Theory they passed our total for only four wickets. There was little noticeable dullness in that match, in which, by the way, I ran and walked over 4½ miles as my share in bowling alone.

In the same month Essex made 196 and 203 for only 4 wickets, again against Fast-LegTheory from both ends.

While, in Australia, the second Test was finished in four very interesting days' play and was won by Australia in a game in which Voce and I bowled 70 overs. *That* was neither a dull nor a monotonous affair.

The fact is that it is, at present, a pure assumption that Fast-Leg-Theory will necessarily make cricket tedious to watch. Only, in my opinion, after a long and intensive trial can that theory be proved or disproved. And, if I may suggest it, there is less chance of *bad* Fast-Leg-Theory being dull than if it is good, because bad Fast-Leg-Theory means run-getting for a certainty, and the people who pay the piper love tall scoring. An ever present fact of cricket this one, in spite of the remark I sometimes hear that "all these long scores kill the interest in the game."

If that is really so why is it that almost the only things remembered about the Australian tour in England in 1930 are Bradman's 334 at Leeds in the third Test and his tall scoring generally, and the Australians' 729 for 6 wickets in the second Test at Lords? I shall have to see a lot more Fast-Leg-Theory before I agree that it spoils the game for the spectator.

A most serious aspect of the case is that whatever the legislation against Fast-LegTheory might be it would encroach upon the rights of the captain and of the bowler.

I ask in all earnestness whether that principle can be admitted *and the game remain Cricket*? To that question there can only be one answer. Another important question is: "What *is* the charge against me?" I have yet to hear a lucid reply to that!

What did I do in Australia that there should have been such unseemly uproars from time to time, that my life should be threatened and that police protection was seriously under consideration, although I was only a simple cricketer from a Notts. village trying to play cricket some ten thousand miles from my home? So far as I know the only charges against me are that because my boots burst during the second Test at Melbourne I kept the crowd waiting a few minutes; that a ball bowled by me in the third Test at Adelaide hit Woodfull who, as the slow motion pictures show, played much too late; and that a ball bowled by me during the same Test struck Oldfield on the head, that player at once admitting frankly that the accident was his fault and not mine. As, indeed, the fact that the ball hit him on the *right* side of his forehead is all sufficing proof for anybody who understands the game of cricket. That fact proves that the batsman had had time to turn his head round and almost to face square leg before the ball reached him; this meaning that he had plenty of time in which to make his stroke. Because, having failed to make his stroke, the ball hit Oldfield is clearly very flimsy evidence against either Fast-Leg-Theory, or the bowler bowling it. To continue the search for evidence against either myself, or Fast-Leg-Theory, on this Australian tour. *Only once did a ball from me hit Bradman.*

That was also entirely due to the batsman's fault, as, in stepping back in trying to cut me, the ball hit him on the forearm: the kind of blow which any regular follower of county cricket sees received half a dozen times a week almost throughout any season.

I ask the world of cricket in all seriousness: "Is M.C.C. to attempt to legislate specially; is the whole edifice of cricket to be shaken; is the game to be revolutionised; are the future relations between the two leading cricket powers to be imperilled on such slender cause as that three Australian batsmen were each struck by a ball bowled by an English bowler?" Really! If certain critics had not made such an effeminate outcry about it during and after the third Test the whole bother would be too childishly ludicrous to merit further consideration by grown-up men. But there is the grave fact that, in a moment of temper, which I cannot help thinking he has regretted ever since, Woodfull was alleged to have said, during the third Test at Adelaide:

"There are two teams out here. One of them is playing cricket; the other is making no effort to do so."

Those words are quite unworthy of the Woodfull we all knew and admired in 1926 and 1930.

I am surprised that he did not at once withdraw them.

The stigma of having uttered them about his guests must remain until he does so.

They are the harshest – and, taking the liberty of speaking for the side for which I had the honour of playing – they contain the most untrue judgment of the M.C.C. 1932-33 team in Australia that any man could possibly imagine.

Such an allegation, even if made by a man in the street, would rouse the dander of a man of straw. How much more marked therefore would be the effect upon the members of the opposing team· when such an aspersion was published and not at once denied by him – as having been made by the captain of the opposing Test team, in whose house we were the guests.

Nor did it tend to soothe our feelings when an Australian paper stated that when Woodfull was hurt the English players gathered round him and appeared to be much concerned about his injury. So far so good. The writer then proceeded "but this was only sheer hypocrisy." That, too, was a statement admirably calculated to make us all feel thoroughly happy and at home among our best friends!

Yet, all the while, there was never a definite charge made against me either of unfair bowling or of bowling at my man. Nothing but insinuation, sneer, and innuendo, anything, in short, to damp the spirit of Fast-Leg-Theory, reduce its sting, and blunt its spearhead.

None dared venture into the open with a fair and square charge against me, or anyone else in the team. So I am left with no alternative but to believe, that if there is a doubt that some of Australia's batsmen haven't the courage to stand up to fast bowling on a fast wicket, there is no doubt whatever that most of those who write about cricket in the Australian Press have no pluck at all. They are content to sneer and jeer at their visitors from their snug shelter behind the screen of either a nom-de-plume, or that valuable title "our special correspondent."

I feel obliged to refer to this matter of a charge against my tactics in the portion of this book that is devoted to the Future of FastLeg-Theory in order to refute at the outset the notion that my bowling is unfair bowling in any shape or form. If I insist still further by quoting from authority the reader must be kind enough to bear with me a little longer.

Thus, M. A. Noble in the *Australian Cricketer,* writing of me and my pace, etc., etc.:

"It is all humbug to say that his tactics were unfair, or that he bowled at the man, instead of the wicket. He didn't."

Have I no right to a perfectly clear conscience after such a decisive certificate from the most trenchant, frank, I might also say biting, writer on cricket among Australians who has every qualification to write about the first class game? Even without Noble's honest "All clear" I am perfectly satisfied, and sleep quite easy o' nights.

Then, I must repeat J. W. Trumble. An Australian of his long experience with no axe to grind, and who is not a personal friend of mine, though I have had the pleasure of meeting him, does not without very good reason write such phrases as:

"The leg-theory attack rather ungenerously called 'body bowling' ..."

And again:

"I consider it (Leg-Theory bowling) quite legitimate and justifiable in Test cricket. It is absurd to suggest that the fast bowler in on-side bowling is deliberately bowling at the batsman with the intention of hitting him."

And again, writing of one of his own innings many years ago:

"I was hit about 20 times all over the body by quick-rising balls. I had also the difficulty to contend with, as in the leg-theory attack, of steering clear of the close-in field waiting for catches. We must take the rough with the smooth; it is all in the game."

Men of J. W. Trumble's stamp do not exaggerate, much less do they lie, when they write of having been hit 20 times.

Yet, compare that one innings with the sum total of "hits" recorded during the recent tour on three Australian batsmen, Woodfull, Oldfield and Bradman once each, and each time the hit was due to the batsman's fault. I claim that these *facts* be given full prominence when the public is discussing me and my tactics in Australia or anywhere else. They outweigh all the adverse statements in the Press, most of which were exaggerations and some of which, I regret to have to write it, were downright lies.

Here I would like to add an extract from a book written by the late W. G. Grace which I read some time back. It deeply concerns this very important subject of physical injury by fast bowlers. In writing about the late Mr. C. E. Green of Essex, Dr. Grace wrote (page 312-313 of *Cricket*):

"I can recall one match at Lords, M.C.C. and Ground *v.* Yorkshire in 1870, when he (Mr. Green), stood up to Emmett and Freeman, on one of the roughest bumpiest wickets we had now and then on that ground twenty years ago. About every third or fourth ball tricked badly, and we were hit all over the body and had to dodge an occasional one with our heads. Shooters were pretty common on the same wicket, and what with playing one ball and dodging another we had a lively and unenviable time of it."

Judging from Dr. Grace's description of that game of 63 years ago it seems to me that Bradman would not have enjoyed playing in it against Yorkshire.

Perhaps modem Australian cricketers, and their idolaters who write in their Press, may have heard of Ernest Jones of South Australia, who was in his day one of the fastest of all bowlers. Indeed, I have heard it said that some years ago when a company of cricketers in Adelaide was discussing the pace of various bowlers, and the question arose as to which was the absolute fastest, someone turned to Jones for his opinion. His reply was laconic and instant.

"Kortright was first and I was second," said he, and went on with his tea.

It is recorded of Jones that in England he managed to bowl through Dr. Grace's beard, and in the same season, 1896, in hitting Hon. F. S. Jackson over the heart he broke one of that gentleman's ribs before he had made many runs, but he went on and made 93; and there was, I am told, little or nothing in the papers about it! In that same year, at Leeds, Jones was so well wound up that the ball was flying round the Yorkshiremen's heads. At last he had the misfortune to hit one of them on the head. Promptly was heard the shout: "Take t' — — off; he'll kill him, and he's got a wife an' two children at home."

Have I not read that in the very first game of the 1905 tour in England, Cotter, of J. J. Darling's third team, hit Dr. Grace full pitch on the chest in the first or second over? It would have been a knock-out for most men. At Trent Bridge they still talk of Cotter's great pace and shortness *on the leg-side* in the first Test of that tour.

As they do of Gregory's performance in the first Test of 1921 on the same ground, when Ernest Tyldesley was struck and was almost carried off the field early in England's second innings; towards the end of which a ball from Gregory touched the peak of Rhodes' cap.

Was there then, or in 1896 or in 1905, so much as a whimper from either the English cricketer or the English Press?

Old cricketers assure me that Jones and Cotter were taken in their day as all in the day's march and I am old enough to know that beyond complimentary talk and writings about their splendid pace and ability both Gregory and Macdonald had an absolutely fair deal throughout the tour of 1921 in England.

On that tour Frank Woolley made 95 and 93 against them in the second Test at Lords and was hit all over the body. There was not a sound from the barracker, and scarcely a murmur from the Press. Frank was even more silent than usual. He, no doubt, *could* have said more than anyone! But in those days Test cricketers did not dash off to the microphone directly the day's play was over to sell their souls and damage the name and fame of the game as being *mainly* a money making machine.

In this important matter I agree absolutely with the Colonial writer who, after observing that Bradman had said before this last tour that he could not let cricket interfere with his business, went on to write that the true answer to that statement is that Bradman should not be allowed *to let his business interfere with the cricket of two countries*.

I have purposely laid stress here upon the deeds of fast bowlers in the past. I have not done so in a "tit-for-tat" spirit, but only in order to prove that very fast bowling *always has been intimidating*. It has always resulted in the batsman being hit more or less and to the very end of the game of cricket really fast bowling will always have that result. It is not in any ruthless spirit that I write that those who are afraid of being struck by a cricket ball should play some other game than cricket. We fast bowlers in our turn have to "face the music." So we know what confronts batsmen who face us.

I have it on good authority that there is some opinion in England which is against Fast-LegTheory bowling. I cannot help thinking that if this is really true, and how it is to be proved short of a vote from the cricketers of England I cannot understand, it is at all events partly due to the evil effect of that detestable, unfair, and inaccurate catch-phrase Body-Line; and partly to people not really understanding what *my* Fast-Leg-Theory is. Quite apart from a possibly large body of opinion against me, upon what grounds, may I enquire, do the antiLeg-Theorists base their objection? Is it altogether because of the fear that the batsman will get hit more often than usual?

If so, to refer again to concise instances, I hit three men in the course of 220 overs in five Test matches whereas J. W. Trumble writes of having been hit "about 20 times" during the course of one innings only, and Dr. Grace wrote of himself and Mr. C. E. Green having been hit "all over the body" during one innings at Lord's.

If the Antis' objection is because they think Fast-Leg-Theory depends for success upon bowling "at" the batsman they can take it from me as a cricket fact that it does not. Not only did I never bowl "at" the batsman, but, the majority of my wickets having been taken "bowled," or caught off balls well off the wicket on the leg-side, or pitching near the line of the leg-side and going away towards the leg-side quite clear of the batsman, the proof is there for all to see that the greater bulk of my wickets were not taken by balls which, had the batsman stood still and made no stroke, would have hit him.

And, what is *really* meant by "Body-Line," and bowling "at" the batsman? Those phrases pre-suppose a stationary target, or how can there be a fixed "Body-Line"? The more so, since the batsman is never still but is for ever walking in front of his stumps. Will the inventor of the phrase, or anyone else, tell me which *is* the "Body-Line"? Is it where the batsman stood originally, or where he is likely to be presently, or later on in the week, or where?! I should like to know so that I may know what it really is that I must avoid in future. I have my own idea that a batsman has really just about as much "Body-Line" as a fast-running rabbit!

I can assure my readers that whether or no a really fast bowler hits the batsman is not in the least degree dependent upon the packing of the leg-side by the bowler. Actually, the converse is truer. The batsman is more likely to be struck when Fast-Leg-Theory is not being practised, since, when the leg-side is packed, the batsman is naturally prepared for a ball pitching more or less on the leg-side. Forewarned is surely forearmed here, if ever.

May I be pardoned for repeating here that when Woodfull got that crack on the ribs at Adelaide I was not bowling Leg-Theory, and, if I remember rightly, there were only three men on the on-side at the time.

Another thing I have heard rumours of, but frankly I cannot believe that any county club could show the white feather in such a way, is that, as a means towards the abolition of FastLeg-Theory some other counties may boycott Notts. and refuse to arrange matches with them or any other county that is believed to favour Fast-Leg-Theory as long as there is any chance of it being put in operation.

Such a boycott would be quite ineffective if its main object was to avoid risk of batsmen being hit. Whether or no Fast-Leg-Theory was permitted, the, shall I say, vicious fast bowler would still get one home now and then, and the last state would be no better than the first! How can such pure accidents as that sustained by George Gunn last season at Trent Bridge be legislated for? The unlucky bowler, Gover of Surrey, was not bowling Fast-LegTheory at the time but all the same a ball from him had the ultimate result of causing George's retirement from the first-class game. Is it to be supposed that if Fast-Leg-Theory was ruled out of the game and I was chosen to play for England next season there would be in consequence any less chance of an Australian being struck by a ball from me? The thing is almost too absurd to be worth consideration.

The thing that really matters, if damage to batsmen is at stake, is the Will of the Bowler. If I chose to run riot, "see red" is, I believe, the better-known phrase, I believe I could hit most batsmen now in the game whenever and if ever I wanted to do so on a fast wicket. And that, too, without a fielder at short-leg.

I am, of course, only expressing my own opinion when I write, referring to the possible boycotting of my county as a likely solution of this problem, that this might prove to be rather a boomerang. The county that boycotted us to-day because its own team happens to be a bit short of fast bowling might have in its XI a world's fast bowler five years hence while Notts. might not. What then? Would that county then ask Notts. for dates? If so with what prospect of getting them?

The truth is that throughout this whole question cricketers have got to take the rough with the smooth, as I fully believe most of us. are always quite prepared to do. The pendulum of cricket is never still. One has but to think of Australia in 1920-21 with a "fast-merchant" at both ends, and England rather short of the real article, and Australia in 1932-33 with Tim Wall doing his utmost against England's array of Mr. Allen, Voce, Bowes and myself. There was no shriek in 1920-21 to abolish fast short-length bowling because Ernest Tyldesley got a crack on the head and Woolley and Lord Tennyson several in the ribs and on the fingers. We just sat tight and watched the pendulum. It swung back all right, as it will again. In 1940-41, perhaps even in 1936-37, English batsmen will be "stepping lively" in Australia, and then my raucous friends the Barrackers, at least, will be perfectly happy.

Summing up the "to be or not to be" of Fast-Leg-Theory, I will be as brief as I can. Fast bowlers are as unavoidably a part of cricket as are slow batsmen.

The game has to put up with both, whether it likes them or not. To the end of Time really fast bowlers will get wickets (i) by sheer pace, (ii) by batsmen flinching at that sheer pace.

Both these things will happen whatever action is taken by any cricket committee.

Sheer pace bowling being as much a component part of the game as oxygen is of the air we breathe it follows that injuries to batsmen will remain equally with fast bowling a part of cricket.

Where the fieldsmen are stationed has nothing whatever to do with the above facts and cannot alter any of them in the slightest degree.

Therefore, as a means for the express purpose of minimising, if not of actually removing, the risk of injury to batsmen any legislation restricting the number of fieldsmen on the leg-side is foredoomed to failure for a certainty. Consequently, in my opinion, any attempt to legislate Fast-Leg-Theory out of the game is a sheer waste of time; while one of such legislation's direct effects will be to discourage fast bowling, of which we are short enough in any case, all over the world. Another, and worse, effect will be to make of cricket a less manly game.

That would be an Imperial disaster.

CHAPTER II

The Australian Doctors' Remedy

THANK GOODNESS CRICKET'S LAWS ARE MADE BY
M.C.C. – A THOROUGHLY IMPRACTICABLE PROPOSAL –
ARE UMPIRES THOUGHT-READERS? – THE LEGAL SIDE OF
THE MATTER – WILL UMPIRES ACCEPT THE
RESPONSIBILITY? – MY REMEDY, IF THERE IS ONE.

My first remark upon reading the proposals of the special Australian committee for the abolition of Fast-Leg-Theory bowling was that Cricket ought to be eternally grateful that its laws are made by the M.C.C.

If George Robey had formed the Australian committee's proposal during one of his lighter moments on the stage the proposal might be understandable. As a serious suggestion by cricketers of long experience it stands for ever as monumental evidence of the absurdities that "statesmanship" *can* produce.

Let me put it this way. Supposing there had been no Fast-Leg-Theory during the last Australian season is it conceivable that, with the expressed purpose of advantaging the game of cricket, a committee of past and present Australian cricketers *could* have produced such an utterly impossible proposed Law of Cricket as the following:–

"Any ball delivered which, in the opinion of *the umpire at the bowler's end*, is bowled with the intent of intimidating the batsman or injuring him, shall be considered unfair, and 'no ball' shall be called. The bowler shall be notified of the reason. If the offence be repeated by the same bowler in the same innings, he shall be instructed by the umpire to cease bowling, and the over shall be regarded as completed. The bowler shall not be permitted to bowl again during the innings."

The Board in adopting the recommendation decided to cable the M.C.C. requesting them to give the proposal their consideration with a view to general application in order to ban this form of attack.

Let me refer to one absurdity at the start. The proposed Law says specifically:– "the umpire *at the bowler's end*." Thus, if the umpire at square leg thinks I am bowling "with intent" he can do nothing!

It is notorious that opinions differ as to whether a bowler is bowling illegally – otherwise "throwing." There is something tangible, visible to the naked eye, even if inexplicable on paper, on which an umpire can form a definite opinion.

But, now, the Australians, bringing the Criminal Code to their aid, ask umpires, who have already too much to do, to turn themselves into "Thought Readers" and judge fairly of a bowler's intent. One has read about known criminals or suspected characters loitering with intent to commit a felony, and getting a few months rest, free of cost, for their suspected intentions. Now, Australia would apply that principle to Cricket!

But, in cricket, *English* cricket, the real cricket, we do not condemn people on suspicion. We want, and must have, definite proof before we condemn. So we demand that before a batsman is out Leg-Before-Wicket not only must the ball have pitched on the wicket but, in the opinion of the umpire, *would* have hit it.

Of course there is not, as far as I can see it at the time of writing, the remotest chance of this fantastic proposal from Australia ever becoming a Law of the Game. But, writing shortly after its announcement in the English Press there can be no harm in it being criticised by the man who is the arch-culprit, the man who is suspected in Australia, and only in that country I believe and hope, of "intent" to intimidate or to injure.

It is naturally assumed that all suggested legislation is always intended, should the proposal become Law, for the good of the game.

I must point out therefore that, so far, the changes in the Laws of the Game – I will not write of any changes in the customs! – which are of Australian origin have been conspicuously unsuccessful, or else inapplicable to the needs of the game in the country of its birth. That is not a good start for this "ThoughtReader" proposition.

The Eight Ball Over has proved to be a farce. Its main result in Australia has been the recording of monotonously big scores.

Covering the wicket was started out there, and if put to the vote in Australia itself the practice would certainly not secure an overwhelming majority – if, indeed, a majority. Play-to-a-finish Tests are a purely Australian adjunct of the game. This notion has its points, which is far more than can be said of this anti-Fast-Leg-Theory proposal. Teststo-a-finish mean in practice that tiring out the bowlers, and that which goes with it, less stroke play, becomes the *first* thing in batting. Is *that* good for the game? Brilliant batting is placed at a discount, while a big premium is placed on the attempting of only the safest of strokes. Is *that* good for the game?

Not content with having Tests-to-a-finish in their own country it is well known that the Australians have done their utmost to introduce this fatiguing form of cricket in England. M.C.C. gave in to the extent of allotting a fourth day for the first four Tests, and, in the event of the rubber being in doubt, the final Test of a series to be played to a finish. I hope very much that this is the last concession our rulers of the game will make. Four days is an ample allowance in which to finish a Test in England in reasonable weather, and for the weather nobody can legislate.

Such a keen and patriotic Australian as Charlie Macartney goes further and insists that three days is ample in England.

So much for legislation of Australian birth. The records show that none of it has been anything like an unqualified success, and such being the case the world of cricket was quite prepared, before the arrival of the latest effort, to look with suspicion upon anything further in the way of embellishing the Laws of Cricket that is of Australian origin.

Now that we have this "Thought-Reader" proposal before us there is more reason than ever to doubt the utility of Australian-born cricket law. Let us dissect this latest effort, or rather let me, who it is aimed to stop more than any other cricketer at the moment, offer my views.

I am fully prepared to admit that the special Australian committeemen completely forgot me and the recent rubber while they were round the table. I am prepared to allow that they were considering only the big, wide, open spaces of the game and the occupants of those spaces. I can picture them saying to one another: "We've just seen this chap Larwood bowling this stuff, and what we've got to consider now – is what his possible imitators may do, and, more important still, how they will bowl it on some of our up-country wickets which are not always too flat, while most are very hard."

If the committeemen faced their self-imposed problem in that mood there is something to be said for the result of their labours. But only something, and even that is very small. Because, in effect, this resolution of theirs gives enormous power for unfair play *on the part of the umpire in lesser cricket*.

The whole world of cricket is well enough aware that the village umpire has been known for generations as "the twelfth man." Some, in fact, style him the best bowler on the side! Imagine then a match between two neighbouring village clubs who have been playing each other out-and-home for fifty years or so. In the Puddlecombe XI "Whizzer" Brown is the star turn. He is the son of the local butcher who is a big-wig in all the affairs of the village, his voice being almost as powerful as Parson's or Squire's. "Whizzer" has been taking his 7 for sixes, 5 for twelves, and 8 for twenty-one with regularity all season, including in his bag a 7 for twenty-three and 6 for fourteen against the deadly rivals from Burtown.

The time has now arrived for the return at Burtown, where John

Stamper, the village postmaster, has stood umpire ever since he came home from the War which deprived him of a leg but presented him with a liver and several well-won medals. Now, Stamper has heard about "Whizzer," and tells his cronies: – "I simply don't stand for knocking folk about." So when the Puddlecombe captain, little suspecting Stamper, puts "Whizzer" on at his end down hill, Stamper's cronies club together and look out for trouble. Sure enough it comes.

Second ball down hits the local doctor a crack in the ribs, which Stamper said afterwards reminded him of Vimy Ridge. The fourth ball caused the doctor's retirement with a broken finger, otherwise the first over had no result. But the second! Having seen the batsman only just escape the first ball, Stamper, to the indescribable horror of every waggon load of visitors from Puddlecombe, "no balls" the second and solemnly notifies "Whizzer" why he has no-balled him. This subdues the bowler for a couple of balls, but, having been snicked for two fours, he tries an extra fast one with the sixth and, this time, Stamper's "No ball!" results in "Whizzer" being compulsorily retired to wherever his captain can best hide him in the field, he being no fielder and not a batsman.

Thus Burtown, with only one wicket down, are relieved of their chief danger, and proceed to make the locally unheard-of score of 143.

Puddlecombe, furious at being "umpired out," do not bat as well as they can, and are dismissed for 95.

So far so good, but while their innings is on Puddlecombe's captain thinks things out, and, like a wise one, keeps his own counsel.

When Burtown go in again he puts "Whizzer" on at the end where the Puddlecombe umpire is standing! Result, 8 for thirty-one; and old Stamper at the other end helpless!

What, may I ask, is the use of this Australian rule in a case like this? A case such as might easily occur in the very first upcountry club match in Australia next season.

Where there is keen rivalry between village or small town clubs such a rule will be worse than hopeless. It would inevitably reduce the local "Derby" match to an affair of reprisals. Would *that* be good for club cricket, which is the back-bone of the game?

But let us in imagination transport ourselves to either Trent Bridge when Surrey are there, or Leeds when Lancashire are there, or Old Trafford for a Yorkshire match, or even to Sydney if South Australia are there and in the running for the Sheffield Shield. Is it to be supposed that either I at Trent Bridge, or Bowes at Leeds, or Old Trafford, or Tim Wall at Sydney, could give of our best, bowl real genuine thrusting stuff *with only one intent*, and that to win the match, if at our elbow is a man who, supposing a batsman plays badly enough to be hit twice, has the power to practically "kill" our careers with a "call" that would brand us for ever?

This fatuous resolution, born of some twist in the brain of a music hall comedian as it might have been, may be O.K. among Australian "amateurs," but I, for one English professional, can tell this very special committee of Australians that we professionals who play for our livelihood are certainly not going to take the risk of being publicly branded as "intentional intimidators," perhaps because an incompetent batsman has played a bad stroke or two.

Have these special committeemen given the legal side of this thing a moment's thought? I wonder. I am no lawyer, but a friend of mine with a legal turn of mind has put the matter to me this way. Say, for example, I am "no-balled" in the fashion provided for by this Australian resolution. The ball which is so "called" happens to strike the batsman, who is a professional, on the temple, or anywhere else, with sufficient force to cause his removal to hospital for some weeks, perhaps months. Cannot he sue me for loss of wages?

The facts are here that the man specially appointed to judge has judged me at the moment of delivery, and *before the injury*, of "intentional intimidation," or "intent to injure," or both. Would that not be damning evidence against me in a court of law?

And what if a batsman so hit happened to die? Would the bowler not be guilty of manslaughter?

Here let me remind the members of the special Australian committee that on the Tuesday of the third Test at Adelaide *Reuter* telegraphed to England the statement that Mr. Justice Sheridan, a leading judge at Quarter Sessions at Sydney, N.S.W., declared that: "Leg-Theory bowling is covered by criminal law, under which it is a serious offence recklessly and wantonly to harm any person, even without malice."

The "calling" of a bowler by an umpire for "intention to injure" the batsman would make things remarkably unpleasant for the bowler in a court of law at Sydney in the event of serious injury to the batsman.

As, in my opinion, and that of every cricketer with whom I have discussed this matter, all injuries to batsmen from fast bowling are *purely accidental*, it follows that if the Australian proposal becomes Cricket Law, then all fast bowlers will have only two courses open to them. (1) Give up the game, (2) risk gaol.

The alleged general approval of cricketers which is said to have greeted this "Thought Readers" concoction in Australia leaves me stone cold. Most of the active cricketers out there know from which side their bread receives its butter and simply cannot give an unbiassed opinion on any official declaration. The sanest Australian opinion I have read is that of A. A. Mailey, who as he has retired from the game is entirely independent of the Australian Board of Control and all its machinations, over and under ground. He said bluntly: "The Board has passed the baby on to the poor umpire who does not appreciate the responsibility," and he doubted if the M.C.C. would agree. He added:– "The relentless, but particularly astute and able Jardine will not allow this modern form of attack, wherewith he practically won the Ashes, to slip from his hands without a fight. His explanation to the M.C.C. should be interesting."

A. Kippax considered the rule will mean the end of Body-Line bowling, while W. A. Oldfield suggested that the rule should apply only to the fast bowling. D. G. Bradman and Clem Hill also gave their full support to the proposed new rule.

One of the Australian selectors, Mr. Johnson, revealed what his knowledge of cricket affairs is by stating that he "expected M.C.C. will accept the proposed new Law."

That opinion alone goes to show how wide apart are the views held on certain aspects of cricket by Australian officials and English cricketers. Take Mr. A. P. F. Chapman's statement for example: "I can foresee great difficulty in putting it into operation. To make an umpire a judge of a bowler's intent is to put upon him a responsibility which I, for one, would hesitate to accept."

I read with much surprise that that fine Australian umpire Bob Crockett is reported in our Press to have said that the new law is a good idea, and that it will not add greatly to the strain or worry of the umpire, ·who should not find it difficult to interpret a breach of the rule. It is all a question of judgment and common sense. The umpire can quickly eliminate any unfairness.

After all, Crockett is reported to have said, "that is his duty, and if the batsman has tried to protect himself with the bat from possible injury from fast balls, the batsman is being bowled at, not the wicket. Setting a close leg field for a fast attack is a barometer of the bowler's intentions.

"I would not watch the bowler but keep an eye on how the ball came to the batsman. A good length fast ball at the batsman's body makes it more difficult to negotiate than a short-pitched ball."

If Crockett did not "watch the bowler" how could he umpire either throwing or "Noball" bowling? If he did not watch the bowler would he not lay himself open to a charge of incompetent umpiring?

Needless to say I disagree absolutely with Crockett that a "close leg field for a fast attack is a barometer of the bowler's intentions" if by intentions he means (as here he does obviously) intentions to injure the batsman. In this sentence Crockett has been either misrepresented or he has shown that he cannot judge Fast-Leg-Theory fairly. I hope he has been mis-reported. His support of the special committee's "Thought Reader" is only natural and can be disregarded.

I mis-judge completely my brother cricketers whether active players or umpires if any of them, individually or collectively, show the slightest enthusiasm for this hare-brained proposal.

However, if by some strange turn in the wheel of chance our umpires are turned into professional "Thought Readers" whether they like it or not, I hope I am there to see the result. I should enjoy watching Mr. Carr if, for example, Chester or Braund was to "call" me for "intention to injure" at Trent Bridge during, say, a Surrey or Yorkshire match. If it was to happen on the first day then there would probably be another instance of a first-class match begun and finished on the same day. And that, too, by a bowling performance!

But, seriously, is it supposed that English captains will stand for this absurdity? If so, they won't act like some of them look. No, I am afraid that after that protracted meeting at Melbourne on Friday night, April 28th, which lasted into the early hours of Saturday, the mountain, consisting of Messrs. R. J. Hartigan, M. A. Noble, W. M. Woodfull and Vic Richardson brought forth only a mouse

It is a great pity. Such a committee having had time to cool down after the storm and stress of the Tests might have done so much. Especially with among its members Noble, who stated about me at the time, as mentioned in another part of this book, "It is all humbug to say that his tactics were unfair, or that he bowled at the man instead of the wicket. He didn't." – and Richardson, who, not only was never struck by a ball from me, but who, throughout the series, was never heard to complain about Fast-Leg-Theory.

Surely Noble did not vote for the "Thought Reader"?

Hartigan, who I understand was Chairman, has no practical knowledge of Fast-Leg-Theory, so that the inference is that the Australian captain's vote went a very long way.

While they were about it I am sorry that these special commissioners did not hit upon what I believe to be the only practical move which *might help* to reduce the amount of, if not to abolish, intensive Fast-Leg-Theory such as I bowl.

This is, to alter the l.-b.-w. to allow of an "Out" decision if the ball would have hit the wicket although the ball pitched off the wicket *on the off-side only*.

If such a Law was in force I cannot of course say that I, for one, would never again bowl Leg-Theory. I am on the field under my captain's orders. If Notts. were playing a deciding, or very important match in the County Championship towards the end of the season and Woolley was not out 170 at one end and Ames not out 84 at the other, and only two wickets were down, and it was a very hot day, well, then, *anything* legitimate remains legitimate. If then Mr. Carr told me to bowl Fast-Leg-Theory I would bowl it. But I *do* suggest that with that ball getting wickets which pitches off the wicket on the off-side and beats the bat fairly, then *all* bowlers, and not only myself, would have so much less need to try elsewhere than good length off-side stuff for results.

There may be nothing in this suggestion but I maintain that it is worth a far more serious and prolonged trial than is the "Thought Reader."

I will now glance at some more of the published opinions on the "Thought-Reader" of leading Australian cricketers.

The one I prefer is Charlie Macartney's "Quite impracticable," says he, as crisply as he used to "tap" me, and not me only, out on the middle. "It would be an awful job for the umpires. They would have to be mind readers."

The reader will see from his last remark why I lean towards Macartney's views.

But I am not quite so much in agreement with him when he says that the difficulty can likely be met by altering the l.-b.-w. Law to read that the batsman is out no matter where the ball pitched, provided the umpire thought the ball would have hit the wicket.

Though I write as a bowler I do not go further than to suggest, as I have done, that it might be the case if Law 24 was altered to allow for the ball pitching off the wicket on the offside only to be a "live" ball so far as l.-b.-w. is concerned. I do not go further than that at present.

I do not think it would be quite fair to the batsman to load the dice against him on both sides of the wicket.

So, let the bowler have the offside and let the batsman take his change out of the leg-side. That, at least, savours more of a fifty-fifty arrangement, and it might be seriously tried out for, let us say, three seasons in all classes of cricket all over the world.

After that, let the cricket Powers meet at Lord's and decide, once and for all time, (i) that the l.-b.-w. Law should, or should not be changed, (ii) that fast bowlers are entitled to have equal privileges with their slower brethren, and (iii) that no Law of Cricket shall be framed which is intended to stop fast bowlers from bowling just they choose, as they have done since over-arm bowling was allowed.

Next to Charlie Macartney I think Warren Bardsley's verdict is the one that "goes." He said:

"Umpires would need the eyes of an Argus and the judicial mind of a King's Counsel to decide whether a bowler was out to scare a batsman. Fancy asking the average umpire to rule whether a bowler is trying frightfulness. I can imagine the brawl that would follow the action of an umpire in disqualifying a matchwinning bowler. The idea is, to my mind, ludicrous and impracticable."

That is another direct opinion to put into the pipe of the Special Committee of Australia, for them to have a good long puff at it.

Mention of frightfulness by Bardsley causes me to comment on the possibilities in specially remembered instances in the past history of the game. Supposing the "Thought-Reader" had been Law when Gover had the cruel luck to hit George Gunn on the head last season at Trent Bridge. Supposing, next over or the one following, Gover had happened to hit "Buster" Keaton, breaking a rib? Gover would surely have come under suspicion of "intent." Yet, so far as intent is concerned, there has probably never been a fairer fast bowler.

Why, on a question of "intent" Gregory would scarcely have survived the first month of 1921, if fast bowling whizzing about a batsman's head and body is to be misread as a bowler's intention to injure.

Another point which has just occurred as I write. In another part of this book I have written about Accuracy in fast bowling. I know that after all these years I cannot bowl a yorker every time I wish to do so. Supposing an attempt to do so results in a full toss on the batsman's knee-cap causing a most painful blow. When he has recovered I try another yorker a ball or two later, but this time, either from getting a little out of step or the ball slipping out of my fingers I bowl just short of a length and, the ball kicking, the same batsman is hit badly over the heart. Would not two successive blows like that justify an umpire in "suspecting" I was trying to injure? Yet, all the while I would be bowling, as always, with absolutely fair intention.

Which train of thought brings me to an expression of opinion that I have often heard and sometimes read. This holds the view that the real danger to the batsman from fast bowling *is in the short-pitched ball.*

That is certainly not the case in first-class cricket, whatever it may be in club cricket.

The real danger of hurt is in the ball pitching just short of a good length, and in the goodlength ball which has happened to strike some inequality in the turf. Onlookers do not realise this. They want to rule out the really *short* ball, probably because they see the batsmen ducking their heads and jumping about, playing bad strokes and making the ball look much more dangerous than it really is.

A typical instance of what I am writing about here was described admirably by M. A. Noble when writing about the first Test match. This is what he wrote:

"Believing that Voce was bowling at the man just before lunch the crowd barracked the bowler when Fingleton, stooping low, allowed the ball to bounce over his head. They were evidently not in a position to judge direction *as the ball went directly over the stumps.*"

Here we have a particular case of the Barracker being entirely in the wrong and demonstrating against the bowler all the same! Actually, in the instance quoted by Noble, Voce had bowled a straight ball. But he was barracked all the same, and this ball went down in the record – and helped to produce the "Thought-Reader" into the bargain – as another instance of the wickedness of FastLeg-Theory bowling!

I hope I have written something here to kill the idea that it is the fast *short* ball that should be penalised.

Above all that it should be penalised by drawing chalk lines across the wicket. That would be almost the last straw. A cricket pitch is no place for a penalty area.

With the introduction of white lines across the wicket there might arise a call for linesmen, as at lawn tennis, in order to be quite sure if the ball had or had not pitched short of the line. For, if a lawn-tennis umpire, perched aloft, cannot always accurately judge whether a *white* ball against a brown or a green background has touched ground on or beyond a white line, it will not always be easy for an umpire, sometimes with the bowler obscuring his view, to be sure where a used cricket ball of doubtful colour has pitched on soil of much the same colour as the ball.

I note that Bill Oldfield approves the "Thought-Reader," but thinks that it should apply only to fast bowling. How he proposes to differentiate between fast and fast-medium, or to distinguish between the two in action, he does not say. I certainly cannot guess.

What is Wally Hammond? Fast enough to be barred and therefore liable to be suspected of "intent," or slow enough to be exempted and therefore to be permitted if he chooses, and the wicket is suitable, to send in an occasional "rib-roaster," as some people call the ball that gets home with absolute impunity? One could pick a dozen or more bowlers who it would take a committee of experienced cricketers more than they bargained for to place in the exempt class. Where, for example, would you put Tate, under Oldfield's rule?

I have seen the statement in print, though I believe this to be without any justification, that Australia has made it a condition that unless the

"Thought-Reader," or some very similar Law, made out specially in order to stop Fast-Leg-Theory, is a law of the game next season, then there will be no Australian team in England.

There can surely be few people who believe that, or who, if such a calamity happened, would not greatly regret the absence of our many Australian friends. I, for one, shall believe it when it happens.

I judge from personal experience on the spot as well as from conversations with men in authority in Australia, both players and journalists, that Australian cricket cannot afford to do without a four-yearly visit by an M.C.C. team. Inter-State matches alone will not keep their cricket mills working full time or anything like it. Therefore, it would be strange indeed if, for want of what most people with whom I have talked about it consider to be a quite impracticable Law, the interchange of visits between England and Australia was to cease. This, however, is a matter for the governing bodies of the game in the two countries to settle amicably, and I have little doubt that sound practical common sense on both sides will gain the day.

CHAPTER III

My Views on Barracking

A NOISY MAJORITY – CAN PAST AUSTRALIAN TEST PLAYERS DO NOTHING? – DRIVEL ON THE STAGE – THREATENING LETTERS – I DON'T "LOOK LIKE" A MURDERER! – A FRIEND IN BENALLA – THE QUORN INCIDENT – A HALF-CHEWED FAREWELL.

"A time will come, a time will come,
When crowds will gaze on the game and the green,
Soberly watching the beautiful game,
Orderly, decent, calm and serene."

A cricket tour in Australia would be a most delightful period in one's life if one was deaf. But, out there, the noisy majority which has nothing to say that really matters, says it so loudly, and repeats it so often, that one gets rather tired of them.

However, the Barracker has had a long innings, the last one very largely at my expense. Off the field he plays me to his own complete satisfaction!

Now it is my innings. As one of his chief victims, I can say a good deal about him. That I do not say more is because really the best retort to such spoil-sports is a contemptuous silence.

Put as briefly as possible the position is that if organised Barracking of the kind that we had to endure at Sydney and at Adelaide in particular, does not cease, there will be, sooner or later, so far as England is concerned, an end of Test Cricket in Australia.

I cannot see any English amateur cricketer going to Australia to endure willingly the outrageously unsporting taunts of onlookers which Mr. Jardine had to suffer on so many occasions on this last tour.

Though an English professional cricketer is in quite a different category, it is probable that most professionals in future will hesitate before undertaking the Australian tour. Those who endured the recent experience cannot be expected to remain silent about the events of a trip which on this one score was a painful disappointment.

That the Australian Barracker thinks himself a rather important and probably a funny person there is little doubt. But I can assure him that the chief effect of his wit has been to prove himself and his kind to be very bad losers indeed. He proved that over and over again on this tour for the whole world to see, and rightly to condemn.

Never more so than during the second Test. Then we had little or nothing to complain about. Was that, I wonder, because Australia won it? But, during the third Test!!

Whether he is aware of it or not, the Barracker has secured for Australia a most evil reputation as the home of bad sports, a reputation which I know full well from personal experience is most unfair to the many splendid sportsmen in that magnificent country. Frank, hearty, bluff, generous and cheery fellows these latter, who, on both my tours I met in every town or city where we put up, and who could never do too much for us.

In my experience there are two Australias, though I can find only one on the map:

(i) The Australia *inside* the cricket grounds.

That is not the real Australia-the one which is on the map.

(ii) The Australia *outside* the cricket grounds.

That, I like to think, is the *real* Australia, the Australia that produced Victor Trumper, of whom I have never heard a word that was not good, the Australia of Joe Darling, of Charlie Macartney, McCabe, Oldfield, Grimmett and Tim Wall, and that perfectly delightful cricketer friend and courteous foe, the late Archie Jackson.

The very mention of the names of such men makes one all the more bitter against the raucous voiced disturbers of the amenities of the "beautiful game with the beautiful name."

Cannot the past great cricketers of Australia lend a hand? Cannot they, for the sake of the country they profess to love, do some thing practical by articles in the Press, talks over the wireless, or by speeches from public platforms-do something tangible to cause the objectionable sections of their usual cricket crowds to call a halt, and to conform more to the needs of those stirring lines:

> *"Soberly watching the beautiful game,*
> *Orderly, decent, calm and serene."*

The Australian Press can do wonders m the same *direction – if it will*.

Instead, on this last tour at all events, it in many places tacitly encouraged the unfair treatment meted out to me and, much more important, to my captain.

Here I must say that in this book I am speaking for myself. Mr. Jardine is well able to take care of himself. If he says, or writes, anything about his unhappy experiences, he will have the full and complete support of his team. If I know him at all, that which he says or writes will be withering, and final.

In him the whole species of Barracker met much more than their match. Which, of course, did not please them at all.

But I hazard the opinion that the Old Player in Australia can do a great deal more than the Press. Or there is nothing in the proposed admiration by the Barracker for his own countrymen, and if that is so, his barkings and bad manners, where visitors are concerned, become therefore emptier still. For so long, however, as the Barracker is encouraged as he is by former Australian Test match players for so long will this blot remain on Australian cricket. The attitude of seeming acquiescence, if not of actual approval, on the part of former "household words" in the Australian cricket world cannot do other than encourage the Barracker.

Sooner or later, as things are, there will be a really regrettable scene. At present, the Barracker thinks he is top-dog. He is justified in thinking so, considering the apathy of officials and the encouragement received from Australian players. It needs very little, only such a not improbable happening as someone to give a lead, for an invasion of the pitch or the pavilion to take place, and to be followed by personal assault. We cannot have been far off some such crisis more than once on this last tour.

Yet off the field and out of the ground what a difference! Except in the Press, to which fortunately I paid little attention, and here and there at a theatre, I experienced nothing objectionable. In my hearing a small child at a theatre, after gaping at me, remarked, innocently enough:–"Why, Mummy, he doesn't *look* like a murderer!" thus rather giving away the show as to the conversation it had overheard in its home circle.

Generally speaking, too much could not be done for us. Invitations were always being refused for us and often hospitality, alike on this as on my previous tour, was quite overwhelming.

Mention of my previous tour, that of 1928-29, reminds me that the Barracker had little to find fault with then in my bowling, although England won the rubber. But then I did not take 33 wickets and nobody on our side attempted a form of attack that was at all events new to Australia. They failed to recognise that I was bowling for England and not for Australia. They might at least. have noticed that essential difference.

If there was any prospect of getting a reply from the community of Barrackers, I would like one to this simple question:– "Would you have behaved in similarly outrageous fashion towards me had I been in Tim Wall's place bowling for Australia?" Such a question needs only Yes or No for reply.

By way of showing the kind of sustenance upon which the howling pack of Barrackers is fed I give a cutting from an Australian paper. It runs:

SYDNEY, Friday. – At Her Majesty's Theatre last night during a performance of "Our Miss Gibbs," Cyril Ritchard won applause with an extra verse, which went as follows:

> *Now this new kind of cricket,*
> *Takes courage to stick it,*
> *There's bruises and fractures galore.*
> *After kissing their wives*
> *And insuring their lives*
> *Batsmen fearfully walk out to score.*
> *With a prayer and a curse*
> *They prepare for the hearse,*
> *Undertakers look on with broad grins.*
> *Oh, they'd be a lot calmer*
> *In Ned Kelly's armor,*
> *When Larwood, the wrecker, begins.*

Money is easily earned on the stage if a singer can "win applause" for drivel of this description, but the mere publication of such stuff shows the readiness of the Australian Press to be nasty if it could at my expense.

It is not surprising perhaps that I should receive threatening letters. There seems always to be a ready supply of half-witted people who waste time and money writing insulting letters. I remember in 1930 when Mr. Wyatt was chosen captain of England in the fifth Test at the Oval that he received a number of scurrilous telegrams and letters, of course, anonymous. Though such things are really very silly, they do not encourage a player to give of his best. Fortunately, for me, I do not mind very much if an anonymous writer expresses a desire to poison me, or considers I ought to be shot and my body given over to the dingoes-if they'll have it. But at the same time it is scarcely the kind of treatment a guest expects in a strange country.

After all, Australia is a strange country to me. This last time indeed I thought it a very strange country at times! But not so strange that I would not return there to play cricket if I was invited, and if the Barracker meanwhile comes to his senses, realises that a cricket ground is not a bear garden, and that if he really wants to howl out loud there are plenty of wide open spaces in Australia where he can exercise his vocal ability without being a positive curse to the rest of the world. It was, I know, reported shortly before I left Australia that I had said I would never return there.

That is absolutely untrue, and the man who started the report knows full well he lied when he started it. I know his name, and I do not desire to sully these pages by mentioning it. He is what is generally known as an objectionable person, and one for whom nobody I know who also knows him has the least use. This is not the first time his lies have given me pain.

But destructive criticism of such an evil as Barracking has become in Australia, gets us nowhere. All visitors hate this thing, and, judging by the spineless way in which Australian officials, players, and Press treat it, there would seem to be no cure. It is certainly not for me to attempt the solution. Let. those who have allowed this hydra-headed monster take charge, get rid of him in the best way they can. A healthy public opinion is no doubt the best way out, but somebody must take the lead, and take it too in no uncertain fashion. It is no new thing. Did not the fathers and grandfathers of the present Barrackers invade the ground at Sydney, to be met by Lord Harris, A. N. Hornby and Ulyett armed with stumps? I seem to have read something about such an incident happening on a bygone day. So that those upon whom rests the responsibility for ending a most undesirable state of affairs cannot plead they have been taken unawares! If perchance the Barracking community said something really amusing or did something to brighten the day's proceedings, there might be some excuse for this growth on the body of Australian cricket. But the howling of rude remarks at the players and the throwing of half-sucked oranges at one another appears to be the extent of their knowledge of what manners on a cricket ground should be. Beyond such a tired and worn phrase as: "Git a bag" roared to a fielder who has dropped a catch, their dense wit does not seem to rise. The only story told of the Barrackers in Australia that possesses a tinge of humour that I know of is one in which the late Mr. J. W. H. T. Douglas figured. It was in a Test at Melbourne. For some reason or other, the big telegraph board which shows the bowlers' and batsmen's figures run by run was not working that day at one end of the ground, almost behind the wicket. Mr. Douglas was bowling from that end and was out of luck. Try as he would he could not get a wicket. Yet he went on bowling, as some thought a few overs too long. At last, during a lull, there came a raucous voice enquiring plaintively:– "Why don't yer have a try from the other end, Johnny? – then yer could see yer analysis!"

Throughout this whole subject of Barracking, it is only too obvious that the Australian point of view regarding what is and what is not Cricket differs vitally from ours. Not only the view of their officials but of their players also. As an instance, I give the facts of two incidents which, I have read, happened when an Australian team was playing in New Zealand. The Australians were 180 runs behind on first innings in their match against Canterbury. They insisted on Canterbury batting again because the follow-on rule in Australia is 200 runs. It was not until the Canterbury captain had produced the support of the committee of the New Zealand Cricket Council to prove he was right in his assertion that in New Zealand they had always adhered to the English rule of 150 runs for the followon that the Australians gave way and the game went on.

The Australians were evidently unaware of the world-wide cricket custom concerning the "rule of the ground" and that it is that which governs the acts of all visiting teams.

On another occasion Australian obstinacy on the same tour in New Zealand was even more objectionable. This time it was at a Test Match. Both captains had mutually arranged all the details governing the match such as boundaries, intervals, and so on, and New Zealand had won the toss. Then, not before, the Australians' manager, who was of course, supported by his captain, said: "Of course, the wicket will be covered every night." The wicket never having been covered in New Zealand cricket, and this matter not having been mentioned until after New Zealand had won the toss and were to bat, the New Zealand captain stoutly refused to entertain the proposal.

Not only would no English side have thought of making such a proposal, but if, having made it, they found their hosts would not agree to it upon such solid and sufficing grounds as those mentioned by the New Zealand captain, the English captain would naturally have withdrawn the proposal.

Not so the Australians. They retired to their dressing room like a lot of sulky boys, locked the door and refused to go on with the game until their demand was acceded to. It is difficult to imagine a team of adults behaving so like naughty children, but that is what happened. Such an incident will serve to show English readers something of the mentality of some Australian cricketers.

In the case quoted here it was some time after the hour for starting the match and the public had been admitted to the ground. So that the President of the New Zealand Cricket Council took the responsibility of advising the New Zealand captain to give way so that the match should take place. Such a state of affairs is inconceivable between the teams of any two countries, one of which is not Australia.

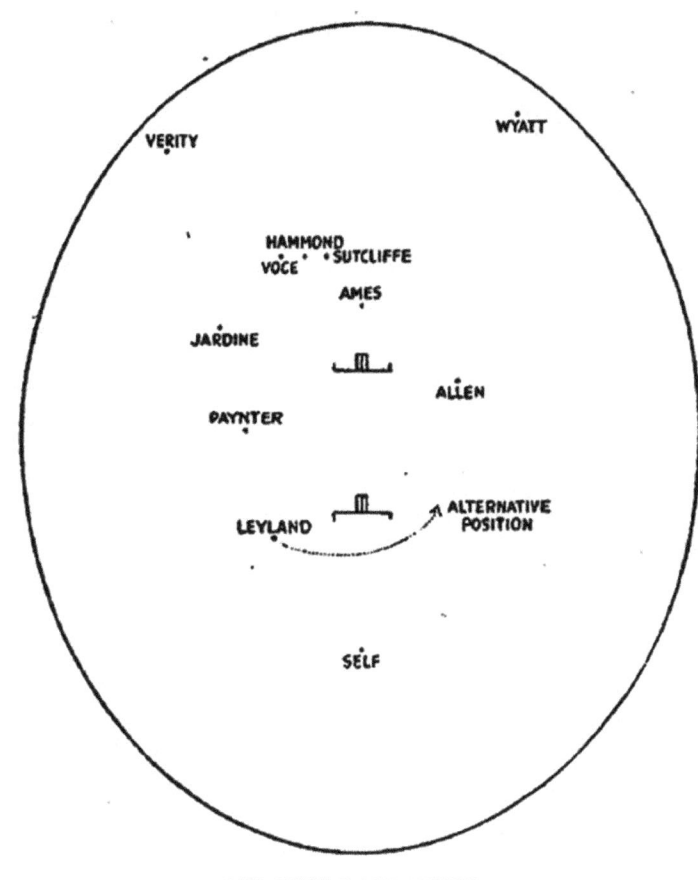

MY NEW-BALL FIELD.

These incidents will give home-staying readers some idea of the kind of things that might happen at any time, and how necessary it is to exercise care to prevent awkward situations arising. They prove how wise was the maintenance of silence on the part of our team even when we were labouring under a sense of very severe aggravation. That we had some friends on the spot is proved by the following remarks which I take leave to cut from the columns of a Victorian newspaper, the *North Eastern Ensign*, which is published at Benalla. My cutting is from an article which appeared on February 17th, 1933, that is to say, on the day following the winning of the rubber in the fourth Test at Brisbane.

The article began:–

"As forecast in these columns some time ago, the victory of England over Australia seemed on paper to be so assured that it was in the nature of taking candy from school children."

It continued:–

"The *Ensign* seems to have been one of the few papers in Victoria

43

which correctly summed up the situation. The problem before the English at the time they left the shores of England was to find some method of attack which might succeed against 'our Don' Bradman who, two seasons ago, stood alone as a world's batsman. He had paralysed all world's records and it seemed that he would reduce the game of cricket to a mere farce. He was in cricket exactly what Lindrum was in billiards. Although special rules were made against Lindrum, the only rule which was carried out in regard to Bradman was to slightly lengthen stumps. (This will be news to my readers. H. L.) The Leg-Theory was devised to stop these countless centuries, and it has proved successful. Amid the welter of abuse and hysterical criticism which has been showered on the English team in general, and on Jardine and Larwood in particular, the following facts stand out:

"That Jardine is the most skilful captain and Larwood the most successful bowler that has ever visited Australia.

"No definite accusation of unfair bowling has ever been made against Larwood. The whole matter is summed up in the fact that Australia has been fairly and squarely beaten, and *we have not sustained our reputation of being able to take a beating in a good spirit*.

"The saddest feature about the whole business lies in the weakness of the Board of Control in allowing the players on the Australian side, or most of them, to rush off to the broadcasting stations at the close of each day's play and bleat yards of tripe through the wireless. It has destroyed the intense reverence that the public had for the secret conclaves which are supposed to be held, and has revealed the distressing fact that cricketers who open their mouths so widely lose caste in the eyes of everybody.

"Cricket reporting should be confined to bona fide journalists who have been in the employ of the leading metropolitan newspapers for scores of years, and not be allowed to fall into the hands of whisky travellers and ex-stipendiary stewards.

"A warning should also be given to parsons, whether they belong to the Presbyterian Church or High Church to keep out of cricket if they wish to keep in harmony with the people of this State.

"We might finally add, in regard to BodyLine bowling, that to those who know *it is impossible to legislate against it*, either by drawing chalk lines across the wicket, or by calling 'no balls', or by raising stumps, or by ordering a bowler off the field, or in any other shape or form whatsoever. And this we will maintain of any body or committee appointed.

"With regard to the fatal cable sent to the M.C.C. after the Adelaide match, it now transpires that this was sent in a moment of hysteria and stress, and has since been bitterly regretted, and the least said about it the better.

"The slow motion pictures which are now being shown at all the cinemas of the two balls which hit Woodfull and Oldfield at Adelaide, reveal the fact that Woodfull was miles too slow in raising his bat and Oldfield walked right into the ball.

"(*Signed*) R. P. L."

I for one take off my hat to "R. P. L." whoever he may be. His article belongs to the scanty list of fair minded statements of what happened in Australia from the pen of an Australian. He does not seem to approve of the cricket writings of W. W. Armstrong, the whisky-traveller, and Clem Hill the ex-stipendiary steward. Personally, I found no fault with anything I read that Hill wrote.

I have asked why the Australian Press cannot do something? The answer is simple enough, except in the cases of such splendid publications as the Melbourne *Argus,* the *Bulletin* of Sydney and the Brisbane *Courier.*

It is: "They don't seem to want to."

To the others the vulgarity and disgusting language of the Barracker spells circulation. They pander to such things because if they did not fewer people would buy their papers.

When I use the word pander I refer to such utterly absurd yarns as that one which alleged a fight between Mr. Jardine and Tate, and that other which said that Stan McCabe had given poor little Eddie Paynter a hiding!

I have hinted elsewhere that the cricketloving English public can have no idea of what goes on in Australia, and how the gutter-Press fosters and encourages the ignorant Barracker to carry on in the disgusting manner in which he behaves.

For example, can any one of my readers picture to himself any English newspaper, even if the thing had happened during an Australian tour in England, giving the details of a fight between the Australian captain and one of his team? I cannot, and I am sure no reader thinks such a thing to be possible. How much more impossible would it be for an English paper to *invent* a scrap between say, Woodfull and Wall, or, earlier, Armstrong and Gregory? Of course no such thing ever happened on this tour as the incidents I have mentioned, but they appeared in black and white in the Australian Press all the same – *to its everlasting disgrace* – always excepting the papers I have mentioned above.

I dare not publish here any of the offensive remarks shouted at either my captain or myself. By far the worst were at Adelaide where, what with their disgust at losing the match, owing to Bradman's failure in Australia's first innings, and the brilliant recoveries made for us by Leyland, Paynter, Mr. Wyatt and Verity in the first innings, and by Hammond, Mr. Jardine, Leyland, and Verity again in the second, the worst specimens of Barrackers tuned up, and considered themselves free to say, and almost to do, anything they liked.

It is while reflecting over the events of the more fiery moments of this tour, that I say with the greatest deliberation, and after fully weighing my words, that it is not worth the while of any English amateur ever again to go on a cricket tour in Australia *unless,* not only has their *present* Board of Control been replaced by one composed of men with knowledge of cricket, and with backbone, but also unless there is a definite official assurance that *Cricket will be played in a Cricket atmosphere.* That is all that the English amateur, for the moment I do not write for the professional, asks.

To use an Americanism, our amateurs simply won't stand again for the offensive, vulgar, and outrageous behaviour of the ill-bred sections of the Australian crowd, in which I include those occupants of the higher-priced seats at the cricket grounds who, for that very reason alone, ought to know better and *ought to give the lead* to the cheap ring, who, in their turn, are not educated by the gutter-Press to learn any better.

I cannot write as strongly as I, and I feel sure all the team, feel over the horrible behaviour we received from the Barrackers, and especially those of Adelaide.

In this connection it is perhaps a pity that Bill Bowes has not published his Diary. Here I present an idea to some enterprising publisher! Bill's diary, published as it is, would be very interesting. I feel sure of that, though I have not read a word of it.

I think I should be off the wicket if I did not saddle the whole responsibility for the evil of intensive Barracking in Australia, which has long since exceeded the limit of what is customary in decent society, upon those sections of the Australian Press and those official cricket bodies, which make not only no serious attempt to stop it, but which, in the case of the badly educated Press strongly encourage it by publishing downright lies, or gross distortions.

That I have ample grounds for such a statement is proved by the utterly untrue telegram from Perth to the Sydney and Melbourne papers, which was sent by some obscure scribbler in Perth. He wired that Mr. Jardine had "no use for Sydney and Melbourne."

The origin of this lie was in the answer of our captain to this reporter's request for the names of our eleven for the match next day.

Following a very old custom Mr. Jardine had replied that he did not know, and that everything depended upon the weather and the state of the wicket in the morning. I believe the oldest living cricketer, except in Australia, will bear me out when I state that this has been the usual custom from the beginning of cricket, but perhaps the Perth correspondent of the Sydney and Melbourne papers knew little about that game. His telegram to those cities makes it appear so. The natural result of this entirely false wire was that those who read it in Sydney and Melbourne were at once made, if not hostile, at all events not favourably disposed towards our captain. Is that either hospitality or honest journalism?

Have those responsible for such a preparation for trouble, such open encouragement of the Barracker, any sort of excuse for such gratuitous preparation of the ground for hostile demonstration against Mr. Jardine or his team? If so, I hope they will produce the explanation, or do the only right thing and apologise to him.

Personally I am content, and certainly happier, in thinking that those sections of the Australian Press which offended did so out of sheer ignorance of what good cricket manners are. I hope that prejudice was not at the bottom of their campaign, since a prejudiced critic is a bad one always, and his writings are not worth the paper they are printed on.

I repeat that I exclude the *Argus* of Melbourne and the Sydney *Bulletin* from every criticism that I have to offer. More so perhaps than the Brisbane *Courier,* but that was probably because Sydney and Melbourne are more in the thick of things and one saw more of their two chief papers than one did of the excellent Brisbane paper.

If I was asked to put the whole trouble in a nutshell I would say that the average Australian onlooker is a thin-skinned bad loser.

I regret that in this category has to be included, as a body, the Board of Control. That body convicts itself of having to bear this reputation by its open support of the Barracker whose general behaviour is wholly different, as all the world can see for itself, when Australia is winning from what it is when Australia is losing. I disagree flatly with Clem Hill when he says that the Australian Barrackers are "the best judges of cricket in the world." Best judges are surely "fair" judges for a start!!

The figures of the tell-tale turnstiles give the lie to Hill.

Let him take the trouble to make a close search and I expect he will find that as much, if not more, money was taken at the gates in about three and a half days at the second Test at Melbourne, *which Australia won,* than was taken in any four and a half to five days anywhere else on this Tour.

It is freely granted that, for patriotic reasons alone, the Barracker does not go to see England win, and that he does not want to see England win.

But it is hotly disputed, and always will be, that the Barrackers and the Australian Press and the Australian officials and players, past or present, who support them have any right at all to be fair to their English visitors *only when Australia is winning*, while retaining the right to behave as badly as only they know how when England is winning.

There cannot possibly be *two* right kinds of conduct round a cricket ground.

The only right kind is the fair kind, that which is fair to both teams in the match.

For so long as men with the influence of Clem Hill continue to assure the Barrackers that they are the best judges, perfect gentlemen in fact, for so long will visiting players have to put up with the vulgarity and hostile attitude which we suffered from. The sooner Australia as a whole realises this truth the sooner will peace return to her cricket fields.

Let Australian crowds learn how to take a good hiding and all will be well with this very vexed question of Barracking. But that lesson has got to be learned.

Right to the very end of the tour I was given cause to remember the Barracker. The final incident at Quorn will show how widespread was the feeling engendered against me by certain writings in the Press. Quorn is a small place somewhere on the map between Adelaide and Perth, and it was my misfortune and that of the Nawab of Pataudi who had the bad luck to be travelling with me – since he at any rate had never bowled Fast-LegTheory, and thus was the quite blameless victim of what happened. There is, I was told, only one passenger train either way every twenty-four hours that thinks Quorn worth stopping at. Were it not that I believe it is not such a bad little spot I should be inclined not to be surprised at this lack of traffic if all passengers get what we got there. It was somewhere between nine and ten at night when our train arrived. The Nawab and I were playing bridge with a couple of Australians and as showing how organised the affair was, I must say that before even the train had stopped our carriage was boarded by a hustling mob of young men and youths for all the world like a Bank Holiday crowd trying to get seats on the last train home. The method of those "sportsmen" of saying good-bye to two of Australia's cricketing visitors was to boo and hiss and, entering our carriage uninvited, to continue a hostile din which really began to look at one time as though, if any one of them had been fool enough to give a lead, it might have ended in a personal attack. We sat it out as best we could hoping the train would not overstay its wait and wondering whether this sort of thing really was to become part of the "fun" of the tour of a winning cricket team! Towards the end of the halt the noise died down a good deal, but just to show they were not really finished with us, these larrikins bombarded us with the pips of pomegranates – which they had been chewing! The name of Quorn has always been associated with packs and hunting, but I take it that the music of hounds in full cry is far more pleasing to the ear than was the discord we suffered from during those horrible minutes.

Which would Australia itself like me, its visitor, to remember? Its warm welcome on arrival in October, its almost profuse hospitality away from its cricket grounds, or the intensely unsportsmanlike behaviour towards me of its thousands of Barrackers, ending with their far from fragrant "farewell, at Quorn?

After all, even a cricketer is human and therefore has a memory.

But Australians can believe me or not, I bear them no ill-will. I might have said a lot when on my arrival at Perth after the Quorn experience, a certain individual accosted me for my "story" of this incident for the Press. But I flatly refused to say a word. It was then he invented the fable that I said that I should never again return to Australia. Whereas, really, nothing would give me greater pleasure than to go out again and make a hundred – perhaps even a couple of them! – in a Test.

For which, if the Fates have anything so kind in store for me, I should no doubt be "counted out" just the same as I was so often on the last tour, during my run up to bowl. If so, then I hope I tire them out!

CHAPTER IV

In re Bradman v. Larwood

DON FINDS THE "EASY-LOOKING PIE" TO BE MOSTLY CRUST.

It was said in my hearing before the last rubber began in Australia that this series was not so much a case of *England v. Australia* as of Bradman v. Larwood.

I mention this because if this extravagant idea obtained in Australia, then not a little of the ugliness that disfigured the struggle for the Ashes is accounted for. Since if, as I say, that idea had general acceptance throughout Australia, where the idolatry of Don Bradman was something that no stay-at-home English cricket-lover can possibly visualise, then Don's failure to deliver the goods on a 1930 basis would so annoy those idolaters that the only object left to them upon which to vent their spleen would be the bowler, or bowlers – not forgetting the captain who used them – who were responsible for that business failure.

Since business failure it was, if there is any truth in the yarns one hears about betting on the game in Australia.

Don played 8 innings against us in the Tests and was once not out.

In his remaining seven innings, I got his wicket 4 times, twice clean bowled. He played on once first ball to Bowes, and was caught and bowled once and bowled once by Verity.

But before the rubber began I got his wicket in both innings in the first match in which I played against him on this tour, that being against "An" Australian XI at Melbourne in November, the first time being l.-b.-w., the second clean bowled.

This second dismissal was described by Jack Hobbs as follows:– "Bradman, drawing away to cut a shortish delivery, missed the ball, which hit the top of the off-stump. What a hush round the ground! In the circumstances, Bradman's attempted shot was bad. He was drawing away, sure proof that he didn't like the bumpers of Allen and Larwood."

I did not play in the match against New South Wales in which Don made l.-b.-w. Tate 18, and b. Voce 23. After this he went for a change of air and did not play in the first Test.

Turning out, as we all hoped, thoroughly invigorated, in the second Test he had the misfortune to snick the first ball bowled to him by Bowes on to his stumps. But, while "snicking on" is sometimes bad luck this was not such a case. Considering that it was the first ball bowled to him, Bradman took a thoroughly unsound risk in attempting the sort of stroke which great batsmen only try when they are set. But I am afraid Don is rather a slave to the "I'll show 'em!" habit. The game of cricket has its own way of dealing with that habit. It is a habit for which English schoolboys have a well-known and expressive word.

Surrounded by his worshippers, Bradman wanted to show them that this English bowling which, they had read, he had clouted all over England in 1930, was quite ordinary pennant cricket sort of stuff, and that his several early failures on this tour against Mr. Allen, Voce and others, were only by way of being slight misprints in his book of cricket. So he failed in his first Test innings and failed badly.

But I award him the fullest marks for his magnificent second innings recovery. His 103 not out was a very fine innings indeed, and I must confess that during its progress I thought at times that he had got the hang of things and might after all successfully defeat our plans. But, and I say it in no sense by way of excusing my failure to get him out in this innings, this was the game in which I had a series of most irritating mishaps with my footgear. Added to the annoyance of having to leave the field more than once to change my boots, an annoyance with which every cricketer who has experienced anything of the sort will readily sympathise, but the severity of which no mere Barracker could possibly understand, I had the skin partly worn off the toes of my left foot. Consequently, I may not have been quite at a hundred per cent in this match. But that does not in the very least detract from Don's innings which could not have been bettered in the circumstances. The next score to his 103 was Vic Richardson's 32, then came Woodfull's stolid 26, O'Brien's 11, and not another double figure. It was a great batting performance on a pitch which, as I deal with fully in the Chapter on the second Test, was not one of the best.

So far then when we faced each other in the electrical atmosphere of the third Test at Adelaide, it was clearly a case of "one up and three" for Don, so far as he and I were concerned. Such an experienced and discerning judge of the game as the former Oxford captain and New South Wales cricketer, Dr. R. H. Bettington, permitted himself to risk the following statement after the second test:

"Bradman's innings is the chief hope of Australia. *He has definitely conquered the LegTheory bowling* and should now make many runs. Throughout the last Test he played deliberately late at good length balls on the leg side. Short pitched balls of any height were hit firmly and never

Bradman and McCabe going out to bat in the first innings, 5th Test at the Sydney Cricket Ground.

reached the packed leg field without first hitting the ground. *He showed complete mastery of all the bowling."*

I did not go quite so far at the time as the Old Oxonian. Subsequent events tended rather to prove that the above, written hot on top of a brilliant innings, and in the flush of a victory of such a character that Bradman was, I was told, kissed once for almost every twenty yards he had to walk to get back to the pavilion, was exaggerated praise. Still, such enthusiasm as Dr. Bettington's about a fellow Australian who, by just winning a Test match, had put his country well into the fight again for the retention, or the loss of the Ashes, was quite pardonable. Particularly when at that moment Bradman's Test match average against England was 103 for 15 innings completed out of 17 played, with an aggregate of 1,545. Since that innings these figures have come down somewhat as, in his next six innings, four of which I ended, Don scored 8, 66, 76, 24, 48, 71, making his present bill off English bowling, 1,838 runs for 21 completed innings, which gives him an average of 87.5. A figure which no batsman should expect to live up to indefinitely. No doubt Don means to make it a treble figure average again next season. The attempt will be worth watching, whether it is crowned with success or not.

In the third Test at Adelaide we all marched into a world of surprises. Quite early we sensed an atmosphere, which rather bucked me up than otherwise for my next duel with Don. To begin with I observed from the pavilion, not without relish, that this wicket which was supposed never to be of much use to a fast bowler was doing something.

We won the toss and Mr. Jardine, Sutcliffe, Hammond and Ames were all with their pads on and off for a beggarly 30 runs.

Cutting out my natural desire for a good score by us this was really a very encouraging state of affairs! When we had made 341 I can say that I never felt better. This was just what the doctor had ordered. So I felt quite strong and hearty when Woodfull and Fingleton came out to bat and my captain put me on to bowl. Fingleton got a touch and, Ames adhering, the first wicket fell at 1. Enter Don.

I was then bowling to a four slips field, as I invariably do while the ball is shiny and likely to swerve away when I bowl it from the right grip for swerve. But since in Australia, the shine wears off much more quickly than it does in England, I soon reverted to LegTheory and placed my field accordingly.

That I did so was at once seized upon by the Press for yet another accusation that "as soon as Bradman went in Larwood reverted to Body-Line in order to bowl at him," or words to that effect.

I need hardly add here, since this book will be read by intelligent cricketers, that had Fingleton stayed another five minutes or so, I should have switched over just the same.

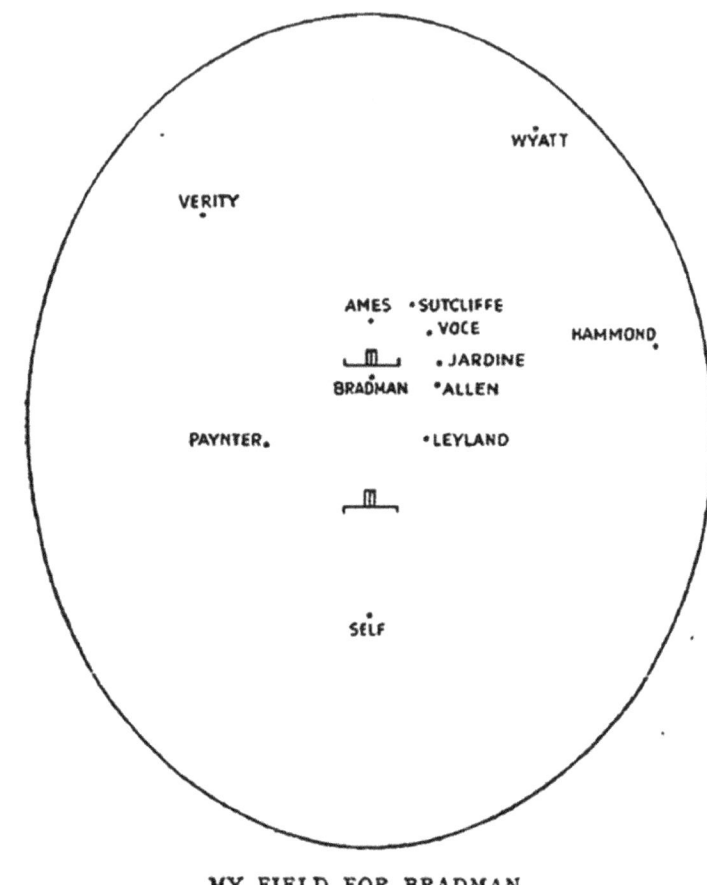

MY FIELD FOR BRADMAN.

My reversion to a leg-side setting of the field was emphatically not done purposely *because* Bradman had come in. I wish to emphasize that as strongly as it is in my power to do so. Australians who do not believe this simple statement are of course welcome to their own opinion.

No sooner had I switched over than Don responded. He is really rather like a young and hungry trout in a pool. The angler does not now even have to keep out of sight! It was not so in 1930. Then he took a lot of drawing. But, on this tour, he rose to the fly much more readily. To what I am to ascribe this change of character I really cannot say.

Was it over-keenness to show that his shocking bad start in the games before the Tests was not his true form?

Was it over-keenness, for business reasons not unconnected with the microphone, his pen, and his friends on the Australian Board of Control, to prove "Australia? It is I!" is his motto. I cannot say.

That row of small scores in 1932 after his terrific scoring in the Tests of 1930, wanted a lot of living down. It seemed to me that in his endeavour to show a sublime mastery of any and every type of bowling which Mr. Jardine could turn on against him, Don was always in too great a hurry. Not once did he play such a sober and sound innings as that one at Leeds.in 1930 when he made fours out of nothing, and when, though he got his runs at a good rate, he always seemed sedate.

This time he was never really the 1930 Bradman. I take some credit for the fact, because I am at present convinced that on really fast turf good Fast-Leg-Theory will always disturb him.

I am perfectly satisfied that he flinches.

As satisfied as I am that I was not completely his master on this trip.

In this third Test it was his departure with only 18 on the board for two wickets when Mr. Allen, who was at any rate deputy G.O.C. of my short-leg squad, caught him off me, that started the Barrackers' orchestra.

The reader must hark back a bit and recall that to quote the unfortunate language which Bradman himself used before the rubber began, viz.:– "We shall be as right as pie at Sydney." Bradman had certainly done something at Melbourne to prove to his vast camp-following that he had not boasted in vain. His 103 not out in that game made without an actual chance, had made the score "one all" and the battle was to be renewed on the Adelaide wicket "which would not help the English fast bowlers." So that when England had totalled 341 and Tim Wall had proved to be the most effective bowler it was felt that only Don Bradman could now make amends. He had done it as promised at Melbourne. He would do it again.

When instead, he was out for 8 and Australia had two out for 18 it was felt by the crowd that not only was victory farther off than they had reckoned on, but that perhaps certain of their financial arrangements in the shape of sundry little side-bets were "down the course" also.

Therefore the Barrackers, already incensed at having been locked out of the Adelaide ground from our practices before the third Test, were in the right mood, from their own point of view, when Woodfull made an inadequate stroke and was hit by a ball, bowled by me when *my field was not set for Leg-Theory.* It was just the cussedness of things that Oldfield should "run into" trouble a little later on, his unfortunately acquired black bruise making everything else look blacker still. Some grand batting in our second innings did not do much to lift the clouds from Australian cricket. Our lead of 415 runs with 4 wickets in hand must have made Don chew the cud a bit about things being "as easy as pie." Hence, his frame of mind when Australia had to get 532 to win in their second innings must have revealed to him that at any rate this particular pie seemed to be mostly crust.

All the more so when I at once bowled Fingleton who had attempted a very unsound stroke. Two wickets were down for 12 when Don came in second wicket down for a change, and our duel was renewed. In this innings he was again brilliant, and flashy in patches. At times it looked like the courage of despair, at others it looked what it was, extremely good, if daring, cricket. The way he was out was typical of his mercurial temperament. He had just hit Verity for six, and not content to wait, he straight drove the next ball. Verity made a very smart catch.

In between that innings and our next opposition in the stifling heat of Brisbane we were threatened with all kinds of frightfulness in the shape of what was called retaliation! As though there is anything novel in *both* teams having as much fast bowling as each can place in the field. We were warned that an aboriginal bowler Gilbert was "half as fast again as Larwood" and that only the season before he had knocked the bat out of Bradman's hands, a thing which I was informed "you at any rate have never done." I replied that the only thing that really interested me was to get the batsman's wicket. I didn't want his bat.

We had a taste of Gilbert in the match prior to the fourth Test, and it was quite obvious that he was only an ordinary paced inaccurate slinger. With such a short run he could scarcely be anything else. True fast, that is to say, *real* speed, bowling is quite impossible from a short run.

Bradman versus Larwood, third Act, opened in a Turkish bath. Brisbane ought to be a good place in which to sink capital in the laundry business, since no sooner has one put on a shirt than it is more or less soaked through, and to wear a stiff collar is torture. But such discomforts did not adversely affect either party to this duel. The keen edge of attack on either side was not in the least blunted by the moisture of the atmosphere, and the "have-at-you" was as fierce as ever. Australia made a magnificent start. When we packed up for the first day with Don the man in possession and 71 to his record I confess that some of us thought the decider would be after all at Sydney, I bowled 20 overs without getting a wicket, Mr. Allen and Hammond 18 each for one wicket each and Verity 22 without tangible result.

When I began next morning, I felt that that was a matter needing righting. So I took 4 for 41 on an even hotter day than the first. The first of these was Don's offstump after he had drawn right away, and *attempted to cut a straight ball though he had only been batting a few minutes.*

Don can never justify a claim to be ranked among the great batsmen of the world, past and present, so long as he is guilty of such fundamentally unsound strokes.

Whether it is sheer funk or not that makes him draw back I cannot say. But I can say that that is the impression which such strokes leave upon any critical and expert observer. My second wicket that morning was Bill Ponsford's. He did the very opposite to Don, shuffling across and missing a plain straight leg-stump ball.

Australia made 340, and I think that between us we bowlers can look upon that day with some pride as we took 7 for 89 on a plumb 'un. So well did Mr. Jardine and Sutcliffe support our efforts that they came back to roost full of pep, and with 99 wiped off.

The next two days were made memorable in Test History by Paynter, as described in another chapter. Not out 24 on the third evening, he made 83, a most courageous wardto-wicket innings as he came direct from hospital each day to bat.

We led them by 16 runs on first innings, and after Woodfull and Richardson had made 46 for the first wicket the duel was resumed. This time, having made a mental note of the attempted stroke when Don was bowled in the first innings, I thought it very likely he would try it again when, as he thought, the right ball offered. And that if he did, and connected, it meant an unstoppable four cut rather square but behind point. So instead of having Mitchell in gully's usual place as a rather square third slip I moved him a little bit nearer the line, of a square point. The oracle worked beautifully! The trout rose to the fly almost as explained in books on angling. Mitchell brought off a good two-handed catch, and now Don was left with only two more chances of consuming the pie easily before his expectant admirers.

And so to Sydney.

I had had six innings at him in three Tests and as I'd got his wicket three times our reckoning was fifty-fifty.

Australia batted first on a really good Sydney wicket, even though it is not now of the run-getting calibre of the old Bulli soil pitches there. Mr. Jardine encouraged me by at once snapping up the adventurous Vic Richardson for a blob, and in came Don.

On his own dunghill so to speak, right in the bosom of his enormous family, since the whole of Australia's inhabitants are as his brothers and sisters, he came to put things right once and for all. His last chance in Australia until 1936-37.

Don came in, I thought, even more slowly than is his wont. The scoreboard read 0 for 1, and he knows as well as anyone the "tail-up" value to any fast bowler of having got that one wicket. He had to take strike.

In this innings he played the soundest cricket he showed on this last tour. He made just over 40 of the runs for the second wicket which fell when I bowled Woodfull for 14, at 59 for 2. And this had been more like the Don I remembered in England. So the reader may well believe me when I say how glad I was when, five runs after Woodfull left, I clean bowled Don again, thus getting his wicket in each of the last three innings in which I had bowled to him. Not "at" him. (Australian papers kindly copy.)

I knew that this rate was too good to last and in Australia's second innings he "had a dip" at Verity, hitting slightly across it, and being clean bowled for the second time in this match. Thus ended the case of Bradman *v.* Larwood 1932-33.

It was what golfers would call a good "blood" match, start to finish. And the shrieks and cat-calls from the gallery probably did nothing to dull the edge of the attack on either side. I was certainly "having at" Bradman's wicket all the time with every ball I bowled. I do not doubt that Don himself was engrossed with but one idea and that was to knock the cover off me.

But from his own point of view he did his, and Australia's, cause little good when he added to his stupid remark before the series of Tests began that "we'll be as right as pie at Sydney," a rather unnecessary taunt to the effect that the public should remember "What I did to Larwood in 1930."

Such things may be said freely enough in the privacy of one's home, or in pavilion dressing-rooms, but, well, I suppose a man can develop a broadcasting mind by a too frequent access to the microphone.

I conclude my chapter on the man who Armstrong rather unfairly dubbed last season a "cocktail batsman" by quoting the pungent remark to me in Sydney of a man I chanced to meet – he was obviously an "old chum." Of course, Don's name cropped up, so did those of Trumper and Macartney. My chance acquaintance summed up these three: "The very shadow of those two on a wall would be worth more to me than Don."

Sydney Cricket Ground

Leg-side attack.
Larwood bowling to McCabe
Leyland, Allen, DR Jardine, Hammond & Sutcliffe

CHAPTER V

The First Test

OUR DISAPPOINTMENT AT BRADMAN'S ABSENCE – A GOOD SYDNEY WICKET AND A GOOD START – FAST-LEG-THEORY USED INTENSIVELY FOR THE FIRST TIME IN TEST CRICKET – MCCABE'S SPLENDID INNINGS – MY TEN WICKETS.

To say that we were disappointed when, with everything ready for the battle to begin, Don Bradman was an absentee, is to express in the mildest manner the real feelings of the English team.

We wanted to win or lose against Australia, not a piece of it.

Whatever his virtues and his faults Don is part of the Australian Eleven, which is unrepresentative without him.

However, owing to a series of circumstances into which it is no part of my purpose to enter fully, Bradman was unable to play. It is really not surprising that his health may have suffered owing to the incessant friction which is inevitable when a man tries to serve two masters. In Don's case it was more than two, assuming Cricket to be one.

Added to his worries due to Cricket, Board of Control, Journalistic, Broadcasting and other contracts, written or implied, was the most important one of all – the one on which all the others depended – viz: that he had so far on this tour completely failed to live up to the big reputation he had well and truly acquired in 1930.

In that failure Bradman saw all his contracts turning to dust. Therefore that failure, for failure it was, *must* be made good. He should have gone all out to do so at the first opportunity.

Personally I don't think that Bradman's trip to the country for rejuvenation was either a good move, or a success. Be that as it may it kept him out of the first Test, for which, considering McCabe's display, and the ever present possibilities in Bradman, we were not ungrateful.

This Test had a special significance, as it was the first in history to witness purposeful Fast-Leg-Theory, in which category I include Voce, since, between his packed leg-side and mine, there is little difference. Actually the only Cricket differences between his attack and mine are that mine is slightly faster while the angle of the two attacks viewed from the batsman's end is totally dissimilar.

To use for a moment the hateful phrase Body-Line, the Body-Line area, if there is such thing, of Voce bowling around the wicket and of myself bowling over the wicket are quite distinct. In those circumstances Voce can pitch off the wicket on *the off-side* and the ball, without break, would go on and hit the batsman if he made no movement. In my case, on a true wicket, a ball pitching off the wicket *on the off-side* can never hit the batsman, and there is little or no likelihood of the batsman giving a catch on the leg-side off such a ball bowled by me. On the other hand such a ball bowled by Voce is most likely to yield a catch on the leg-side.

The Fast-Leg-Theory of the pair of us is practically alike when Voce bowls over the wicket. Then, his left hand delivers much nearer the point from which my right hand lets the ball go.

Thus, when Voce is bowling over the wicket and is sharing the bowling with me the batsmen are enjoying double Fast-Leg-Theory. This they did frequently throughout the last rubber. It was this attack that Mr. Jardine chose with which to open the campaign. That his judgment would seem to have been accurate the result shows, as between us we took 9 of the first innings wickets, and 7 in the second innings. So that the first Test was a great match for my county, with 16 out of the 20 wickets.

Larwood to Ponsford with a Body-Line field

England made a most encouraging start with Woodfull out at once and Fingleton well caught by Mr. Allen off me, and Kippax l.-b.-w. to me before 70 was on the board. Mr. Jardine showed his hand at once with frequent changes of bowling, his first three, for example, being at 10, 22, and 28. I am not writing for or against these tactics when I say that what suits one eleven will not necessarily suit another. I can only say it suited me down to the ground, as I kept on going on after a rest, with a spurt of sometimes only three overs, stepping on the gas every time.

The result of the first day's play was that we had six of them out for 290, but McCabe was one of the remaining four.

Next day he played as good cricket as one could wish to see, getting on his toes to the shorter ones and clipping them safely between our packed leg-side or flicking the off-ball with a crisp certainty that augured as well for Australia in the matches to come as it looked unappetising for us. We had expected normal improvement on the McCabe of 1930 but we scarcely expected such a masterly mixture of pugnacious attack and plucky defence.

This innings can always be referred to with assurance by the many believers in Fast-LegTheory as sufficing proof that it is not physically dangerous and that it can be both played and scored off. After, all bowlers are mortal and whatever their tactics must bowl some bad length balls!

The beginning of our innings gave past and present Australian cricketers plenty of stuff to chew. They knew before the Tests began that our batting was pretty useful. Now, in their first innings, our bowling had proved to be much more formidable than expected, since nine of their men had made only 153 on a good Sydney wicket. This was followed by our 100 up and our first pair still there!

This performance of Mr. Wyatt's is, I understand, a record, in that in his first first-wicket partnership in a Test he helped to put up three figures. If he had only got the pace of the ground quicker on this tour he would have nigh doubled his aggregate. But he played across a bit at first, and rather invited the leg-before decisions that were showered on him. I am not saying that all were out or not. *Onlookers cannot judge of this in any case*, and all umpires make mistakes.

The Australians thus had Sutcliffe and Hammond well set, nearly 300 on the board, and the Nawab of Pataudi, Mr. D. R. Jardine, and Ames still to go in before some of us longhanders, occupants of what some folk call the "hutch," were ready to give battle. The outlook for them was unsettled when play was resumed, but they faced it with characteristic coolness. Actually they let us make only 227 more in a full day's play. The Nawab of Pataudi's quite natural anxiety to get a hundred in his first Test helped to slow down the rate of scoring which Sutcliffe had already set. Even Hammond got his runs slower than usual. But some of this slowness was due to the batsmen's anxiety to have a good look at O'Reilly and Nagel. Tim Wall was not a novelty, Grimmett and McCabe they knew more or

less by heart, but the longer they stayed the more likely were they to discover every asset in O'Reilly's bank. Nagel having to his credit that Melbourne performance, when we were all out for 60, it was the right game to do everything to prevent a repetition while at the same time finding out all there is to know about his bowling. The result was 2 for 110 in his 43 overs, but they were a good two, Hammond and the Nawab.

O'Reilly's 3 for 117, not much to look at, was a better performance, and all the time he was on he looked like a bowler.

We led them by a cool 164 runs, and from the moment I bowled Woodfull for a duck and Voce bowled Bill Ponsford for 2, it was a winning game all the way. When Voce was proving ineffective Wally Hammond chipped in with the most useful wickets of McCabe and the dangerous Richardson, and, in the end, we had them out with the scores at tie.

Only one spectator on the famous "Hill" came to see England score one run to win – a good sport that!

I was very pleased to bring off such a double as 5 for 96 and 5 for 28 on the Sydney ground as, on the previous tour, I had sad recollections of the only Test played there. In the first at Brisbane I had taken altogether 8 for 62 so that 4 for 182 at Sydney in the next Test was disheartening. But now, thanks to the thoughtful help I received from my captain, I hope I have wiped that slate clean.

Mr. Allen's bowling was strangely ineffective in this Test. In seeking for an explanation of this phenomenon the only one I have to offer, and I have not discussed the point with Mr. Allen, is that he was handicapped by the unfair accusations made in print by Armstrong and Noble before the Test began.

Both hinted bluntly that Woodfull would be justified in objecting to Mr. Allen's "follow up," as he cut up the wicket.

Armstrong stated that England "take a grave risk" if they play Mr. Allen as, said he, if they play him "they will be unable to bowl him"!!

He went on to express his surprise that Mr. Jardine had permitted Mr. Allen to bowl against New South Wales, and expressed his opinion that both Messrs. A. C. MacLaren and F. S. Jackson would have taken Mr. Allen off immediately.

The value of such partisan criticism is nil.

Its probable object was to put both the bowler and his captain off.

How senseless it was is proved by the facts that Mr. Allen bowled in Australia exactly as he has bowled for many years in England against all the counties played by Middlesex, against the Australian XI of 1930, against the New Zealand XI of 1931, against the Players, and for Cambridge University against Oxford University. Mr. Allen has bowled for over ten seasons in such company, *without ever a murmur of objection from an opposing captain, or player, or umpire, or critic in the Press.*

Are all these people blind or incompetent, and only Armstrong and Noble capable of judging? Or are Messrs. Jardine and Allen thoroughly bad sportsmen?!

One is left with the impression that Armstrong's criticism was a mixture of gratuitous nonsense and desire for sensationalism in print. Assessed lightly, it was grossly unfair to a visiting bowler on the eve of a Test match. I was not surprised to find on my return to England that every cricketer and lover of the game that I have met greatly resented it. I refrain from attempting to express here what our team thought of it all.

It was deeply regretted, too, that such a sane judge and critic as M. A. Noble should have allowed himself to write:

"Voce and Allen must expect a strong protest from Woodfull to the Test umpires if the bowlers persist in their previous tactics ..."

Noble wrote that after stating:

"I have inspected the wicket following the New South Wales game, and found it in a shocking condition; a state of affairs that should be easily avoidable."

Now, I maintain that it is open to question if writers are playing the game – and especially writers with the authority attaching to the names of past Australian captains – when they write phrases which *may* be read in the light of tacit advice to their own captains and umpires to "stop" an opponent bowler from playing his part.

All such things as those referred to by Armstrong and Noble are exclusively the province of the opposing captain and the umpires.

These need no telling from onlookers as to whether or not a bowler is cutting up the wicket.

Is it not possible also that some of the "shocking condition" of the Sydney wicket at which Noble expresses such pious horror was caused by the soles and nails of Australian cricketers? A very little thought would have shown him that such was the case, and would have caused him to modify considerably a criticism that was as offensive as it was unfair to men who were Australia's guests.

But I am afraid the ordinary courtesies of every-day life do not carry much weight with the majority of Australian cricketers where actual play is concerned. To them Cricket is War, and should be waged as such. They are a little apt to bow down to the often-quoted saying: "Necessity hath no law."

Thus, their covert appeal to the umpires and to Woodfull in this alleged cutting up of the wicket was in the light of a hint that it was necessary for fair play that the alleged cutting-up should be put a stop to.

As there *was* actually no avoidable cutting-up, all the special pleading of Armstrong and Noble was so much nonsense. It was what the Americans call "blah." A certain amount of cheery "blah" in life is harmless, but when it is published where and at the time that this was published it becomes something serious.

That aside, it showed that cricket journalism is best left to cricket journalists. We in England sometimes read some more or less accidental absurdities in print, but, at any rate, they are seldom unfair, and never so *to members of visiting teams.*

First Test

AUSTRALIA

First Innings		Second Innings	
W. M. Woodfull, c. Ames, b. Voce	7	b. Larwood	0
W. H. Ponsford, b. Larwood	32	b. Voce	2
J. H. Fingleton, c. Allen, b. Larwood	26	c. Voce, b. Larwood	40
A. F. Kippax, l.-b.-w., b. Larwood	8	b. Larwood	19
S. J. McCabe, not out	187	l.-b.-w., b. Hammond	32
V. Y. Richardson, c. Hammond, b. Voce	49	c. Voce, b. Hammond	0
W. A. Oldfield, c. Ames, b. Larwood	4	c. Leyland, b. Larwood	1
C. V. Grimmett, c. Ames, b. Voce	19	c. Allen, b. Larwood	5
L. Nagel, b. Larwood	0	not out	21
W. J. O'Reilly, b. Voce	4	b. Voce	7
T. W. Wall, c. Allen, b. Hammond	4	c. Ames, b. Allen	20
Byes, 12; l.-b., 4; n.-b., 4	20	Byes, 12; l.-b., 2; n.-b., 2; w., 1	17
Total	360	Total	164

FALL OF WICKETS

First Innings

1	2	3	4	5	6	7	8	9	10
22	65	82	87	216	231	299	300	305	360

Second Innings

1	2	3	4	5	6	7	8	9	10
2	10	61	61	101	104	105	113	151	164

BOWLING ANALYSIS

First Innings

	O.	M.	R.	W.		O.	M.	R.	W.
Larwood	31	5	96	5	Verity	13	4	35	0
Voce	29	4	110	4	Hammond	14.2	0	34	1
Allen	15	1	65	0					

Second Innings

	O.	M.	R.	W.		O.	M.	R.	W.
Larwood	18	4	28	5	Hammond	15	6	37	2
Allen	9	5	13	1	Verity	4	1	15	0
Voce	17.3	5	54	2					

ENGLAND.—First Innings

Sutcliffe, l.-b.-w., b. Wall	194
R. E. S. Wyatt, l.-b.-w., b. Grimmett	38
Hammond, c. Grimmett, b. Nagel	112
The Nawab of Pataudi, b. Nagel	102
Leyland, c. Oldfield, b. Wall	0
D. R. Jardine, c. Oldfield, b. McCabe	27
Verity, l.-b.-w., b. Wall	2
G. O. Allen, c. and b. O'Reilly	19
Ames, c. McCabe, b. O'Reilly	0
Larwood, l.-b.-w., b. O'Reilly	0
Voce (not out)	0
Byes, 7; l.-b., 17; n.-b., 6	30
Total	524

Second Innings.—Sutcliffe, not out 1: Wyatt, not out 0 Total (no wkt.), 1.

FALL OF WICKETS
First Innings

1	2	3	4	5	6	7	8	9	10
112	300	423	423	470	479	518	522	522	524

BOWLING ANALYSIS
First Innings

	O.	M.	R.	W.		O.	M.	R.	W.
Wall	38	4	104	3	Grimmett	64	22	118	1
Nagel	43.4	9	110	2	McCabe	15	2	42	1
O'Reilly	67	32	117	3	Kippax	2	1	3	0

Second Innings

	O.	M.	R.	W.
McCabe	0.1	0	1	0

CHAPTER VI

The Second Test

THAT WICKET – THE TRUTH ABOUT IT – O'REILLY·TAKES HIS PLACE AMONG TEST RANK BOWLERS – OH! FOR A PAIR OF BOOTS.

Although I think we were well satisfied with our victory in the first Test after losing the toss, it was only natural we should remember when we reached the Melbourne ground on the first morning of the SECOND TEST that Bradman did not play in the first and that he was playing in this one.

Consequently, it was anxiously we looked at the wicket, after having heard a rumour that it wasn't looking quite as well as we were accustomed to see wickets in Australia look before the toss. We could not help recalling that it was here that Nagel had got us out in the second innings of the "An" Australian match in November, and though he was not to play in this Test there were others like O'Reilly and Ironmonger who we knew could turn the ball to some purpose. The Melbourne wicket is the worst in the wide world after rain and sun, so our feelings can be guessed at when on inspection the pitch did not meet with our unanimous approval.

There were cracks in it *before a ball had been bowled*.

I have read reports from accredited writers on the game which stated it was a perfectly good wicket. Why anyone should write such a statement, which is directly contrary to the facts, I do not understand.

I am not stating that it was a bad wicket, still much less do I wish to be understood to blame the pitch for our defeat. But it was quite definitely the kind of wicket upon which it is far better to have the runs in the book than to have to make them.

In addition to the cracks which one would naturally expect not to close during the course of play, the pitch was not quite as hard as one expected to find, which fact justified the belief that the watering of it might have been more accurately timed. I make no accusation of purposeful slowing down of the turf to assist in "killing" our fast-bowling attack, but I do think, and I am not alone in thinking it, that when a Test match is afoot a good deal more care should be taken in the "timing" of the watering of the wicket than obviously had been exercised in this instance.

Writing generally of the wickets at Sydney, Melbourne and Adelaide, there is no doubt whatever that all were different, and noticeably slower, than when I was in Australia in 1927-28. I wonder how this happened, and if it would have happened had Australia possessed last season a Gregory or a Macdonald?!

Well, the time came to toss and when Woodfull spun the coin the faces of both captains were being read by many anxious eyes as the coin fell. Mr. Jardine lost, and we were soon busy on Woodfull and Fingleton who, in Ponsford's absence, the Australian captain had taken in with him.

I noticed with pleasure that for the first time in his Test career Woodfull did not take first ball. This may have been due to his desire to "blood" Fingleton, but I think not. Mr. Allen bowled Woodfull at 29, and O'Brien, a left-hander, was wisely sent in to assist in Australia's main job, which was to tire the fast stuff.

But it is a job indeed to tire *four* fast stuffs, with such a good length bowler of some pace as Hammond to give the batsmen very little help in between. O'Brien, fortunately for us, was run out at 67. That was pleasing enough but our content may be imagined when Don Bradman, attempting an absolutely unsound stroke at the first ball bowled to him, snicked it into his wicket. 67 for 3, and one of those three Bradman, put us in grand spirit. Once more we had made a good start and from that we never really looked back in this innings. We had 7 of them out for 194 on the first day, Mr. Allen and "Tangy" Voce bowling magnificently.

I could do nothing, and had to content myself next day with the two worst wickets on the side, those of O'Reilly and Ironmonger.

Woodfull ducking to a plain straight ball from Larwood

69

But, so terrible is Fast-Leg-Theory bowling, I can say that though there were cracks in the wicket and Australia's picked eleven was out for such a total as 228 none of their batsmen had been maimed by it!

On the second day, after we had finished off their innings for 34 more runs, we should have been badly in the cart but for Sutcliffe's 52 and a plucky 26 not out from Mr. Allen. Sutcliffe was not at his best and was bothered by O'Reilly. This bowler proved himself Test class by making the fullest use of anything the pitch had to offer. He hit the wood three times, and got Mr. Wyatt leg before which is much the same thing as hitting the wicket. We had 9 down for 161, upon which, and the lively prospect of fourth innings, we had to brood over the week-end. There were also clouds in the offing, and altogether it needed all the cheerfulness of our invaluable skipper, and imperviousness to anything like gloom on the part of Messrs. Brown and Allen and that cheery Derbyshire lad Mitchell, not forgetting Maurice Tate's immovable smile, to help us keep the old flag flying.

On the Monday O'Reilly finished the innings by getting Mr. Allen caught and Australia had the priceless lead of 59 runs upon which to build up. While O'Reilly took 5 for 63, Wall bowled very well for his 4 for 52. Though Ironmonger did not get wickets he kept hitting a length for 14 overs off which we could only muster 28 runs.

We again got a good start when Ames caught Fingleton off Mr. Allen with only one run on the board. I got past O'Brien's defence at 27 for 2 and Bradman strolled in. The back of Australia was broken when at 78 Mr. Allen caught Woodfull off me, and three runs later he bowled McCabe all over his wicket. To get McCabe for 32 and 0 after his great innings at Sydney was most encouraging. But there was still Don at one end and, as I have written elsewhere in this book, he was this time more like the 1930 vintage. His was a grand innings, and though I don't think any innings can be bad enough to justify the player of it being punished by being embraced on his way back to the pavilion, there is no doubt it deserved most of the praise bestowed on it.

While we hammered away at the other end, getting wickets at such regular intervals as 131, 156, 188, 194, 200, 222 and 228, Bradman was impervious. He played me better than at any other period of the tour.

Wally Hammond did a good job, getting 3 for 21 in 10 overs and again Voce bowled better than his figures.

I am not to be considered as expressing an opinion on the vexed question of who was the best partner for Sutcliffe when I say that Mr. Jardine's decision to send Leyland in with him on the third evening paid handsomely. We had 251 to get to win and these two returned undefeated with 43 of those arrears wiped off. Without rain there was a good look about the match when we went to bed. But cricket always keeps one guessing, and next day, what with the good bowling-and the flies! – we were all out 139, O'Reilly confirming previous impressions with 5 for 66, and Ironmonger 4 for 26, doing practically all the damage. Poor Clarry Grimmett had 1 for 21 and 0 for 19 as his share of Australia's only victory, and as he scored only 2 and 0 it was generally felt that this was probably his final Test. But he was given one more spin at Adelaide where he got three very expensive wickets and was not seen again. I should not like to say that this popular little fellow will never bowl again in a Test. He might still get really good analyses on our pitches, and the famine in bowling in Australia may yet force him into the next side. I feel that every cricketer in England will regard it as a strange Australian team if the little South Australian is not in it, and all will genuinely regret his absence should it befall. For he is a good lad, who never ruffled anyone. He might almost be an Englishman, he is so popular in England.

The result of this game made the rubber "one all" and three to play. It also helped to fog certain watchers, Dr. Bettington in Australia stating that Bradman had "definitely conquered the Leg-Theory bowling," and a writer in a London paper deciding that "it only needs Bradman and McCabe to get set in one of the remaining Test matches for the poverty of the Leg-Theory to be thoroughly exposed!" As to this, I may say that in those remaining Tests I got 19 wickets for 418 runs, 22 runs per wicket. So the real exposure has yet to come, anything under 30 runs per wicket being usually considered fairly good, and under 25 very good going on Australian wickets. We went on to Adelaide unshaken in our belief that we were the better side, but a little bit doubtful of the result of the next Test because Adelaide had the reputation of being the grave of English hopes, as its wicket was supposed to be "no good for fast bowlers," and because of our natural respect for Bradman's ability now that he had, to all appearances, got going again. It never pays to undervalue your opponent.

Second Test

AUSTRALIA

First Innings		Second Innings	
J. H. Fingleton, b. Allen	83	c. Ames, b. Allen	1
W. M. Woodfull, b. Allen	10	c. Allen, b. Larwood	26
L. P. O'Brien, run out	10	b. Larwood	11
D. G. Bradman, b. Bowes	0	not out	103
S. J. McCabe, c. Jardine, b. Voce	32	b. Allen	0
V. Y. Richardson, c. Hammond, b. Voce	34	l.-b.-w., b. Hammond	32
W. A. Oldfield, not out	27	b. Voce	6
C. V. Grimmett, c. Sutcliffe, b. Voce	2	b. Voce	3
T. Wall, run out	1	l.-b.-w., b. Hammond	0
W. J. O'Reilly, b. Larwood	15	c. Ames, b. Hammond	0
H. Ironmonger, b. Larwood	4	run out	0
Byes, 5; l.-b., 1; n.-b., 2; w., 2	10	Byes, 3; l.-b., 1; n.-b., 1; w., 4	9
Total	228	Total	191

FALL OF WICKETS

First Innings

1	2	3	4	5	6	7	8	9	10
29	67	67	131	156	188	194	200	222	228

Second Innings

1	2	3	4	5	6	7	8	9	10
1	27	78	81	135	150	156	184	186	191

BOWLING ANALYSIS

First Innings

	O.	M.	R.	W.		O.	M.	R.	W.
Larwood	20.3	1	52	2	Hammond	10	3	21	0
Voce	20	3	54	3	Bowes	19	2	50	1
Allen	17	3	41	2					

Second Innings

	O.	M.	R.	W.		O.	M.	R.	W.
Larwood	15	2	50	2	Voce	15	2	47	2
Allen	12	1	44	2	Hammond	10.5	2	21	3
Bowes	4	0	20	0					

ENGLAND

First Innings		Second Innings	
Sutcliffe, c. Richardson, b. Wall	52	b. O'Reilly	33
R. E. S. Wyatt, l.-b.-w., b. O'Reilly	13	l.-b.-w., b. O'Reilly	25
Hammond, b. Wall	8	c. O'Brien, b. O'Reilly	23
The Nawab of Pataudi, b. O'Reilly	15	c. Fingleton, b. Ironmonger	5
Leyland, b. O'Reilly	22	b. Wall	19
D. R. Jardine, c. Oldfield, b. Wall	1	c. McCabe, b. Ironmonger	0
Ames, b. Wall	4	c. Fingleton, b. O'Reilly	2
G. O. Allen, c. Richardson, b. O'Reilly	30	st. Oldfield, b. Ironmonger	23
Larwood, b. O'Reilly	9	c. Wall, b. Ironmonger	4
Voce, c. McCabe, b. Grimmett	6	c. O'Brien, b. O'Reilly	0
Bowes, not out	4	not out	0
Bye, 1; l.-b., 2; n.-b., 2	5	Leg-byes, 4; n.-b., 1	5
Total	169	Total	139

FALL OF WICKETS

First Innings

1	2	3	4	5	6	7	8	9	10
30	43	83	98	104	110	122	138	161	169

Second Innings

1	2	3	4	5	6	7	8	9	10
53	53	70	70	77	85	135	137	138	139

BOWLING ANALYSIS

First Innings

	O.	M.	R.	W.		O.	M.	R.	W.
Wall	21	4	52	4	Grimmett	16	4	21	1
O'Reilly	34.3	17	63	5	Ironmonger	14	4	28	0

Second Innings

	O.	M.	R.	W.		O.	M.	R.	W.
Wall	8	2	23	1	Ironmonger	19.1	8	26	4
O'Reilly	24	5	66	5	Grimmett	4	0	19	0

CHAPTER VII

The Third Test

THE "ATMOSPHERE" MATCH – SIX DAYS' TENSION – AN ATTACK OF HYSTERIA –BATSMEN UNLUCKILY HIT – SPLENDID BATTING BY LEYLAND, PAYNTER AND MR. WYATT – DID IRONMONGER USE RESIN, OR EUCALYPTUS OIL? – FAST BOWLING AGAIN BEATS AUSTRALIA.

Only two of the five Tests on this Tour went into the sixth day and the Third was one of them. To be quite honest most of us could have done without some of those six days. There was an "atmosphere" before Mr. Jardine won the toss. That was because, two evenings before, large numbers of people had come to the Adelaide ground where both teams were exercising at the nets. They had made of our net practice an object of derision and they gave an exhibition of bad manners, some if not all of it aimed at our Captain, which would have justified him in having nothing further to do with the tour.

But Mr. Jardine has a way with him in the face of serious provocation of the most irritating kind which is beyond any praise that I am able to bestow. He could not stop the rowdiness, but of course the move to end it should have come from the Board of Control or its representative on the spot. I will give the powers this much credit that they did decide to close the ground next day so that we were able to have our nets in peace. The whole of this outbreak was uncalled for and quite unprovoked. The scoffers had not even the excuse that I was bowling LegTheory, or that some incompetent batsman had been struck by the ball. They had not even the excuse that the Australian XI was getting another good hiding to enrage them. There was absolutely no justification for the bad behaviour of those who paid nothing to come and give this exhibition of bad manners. It seemed to be all part of an organised campaign against us.

Shutting out the crowd gave us a quiet day before the Test for which all of us were very grateful, but it also put many of them in the right mood for a row when play began. This it did on a wicket that looked so good that we were glad when Mr. Jardine won the toss. But it was plain before long that the pitch was not true. The ball flew a bit, and when Mr. Jardine's leg stump was hit, to the undisguised joy of the rowdy ones, and Hammond, never comfortable, was out at 16, I was sorry I was not bowling. Sutcliffe was taken at short leg and with Ames bowled by a faster one from Ironmonger we lunched on the unpalatable appearance of a score of 37 for four wickets. If ever a match looked lost in the before-lunch spell of the first day this one did, because they were four such good wickets that had gone.

On resuming, Leyland went for the bowling and with Mr. Wyatt's defence impregnable things looked much better. The pair added over 100 for the fifth wicket and still went on until they had actually added 156 runs. This was one of the finest partnerships in a losing cause that I can remember.

It was during this partnership that Leyland, suspecting that Ironmonger was using resin on his fingers in order to make the ball spin more, spoke to that bowler, and Woodfull was called in. Upon Ironmonger showing that he had no resin Leyland was satisfied. I read afterwards that Ironmonger had eucalyptus oil on his handkerchief to help in warding off the flies. If that is so, we did not know then that eucalyptus oil rubbed on leather tends to make it sticky!!

Leyland played on to O'Reilly at 186 and ten runs later, Paynter being in, Mr. Wyatt's priceless 78 came to an end when Vic Richardson caught him at mid-off. At close of play Paynter 25 and Verity were in charge, Mr. Allen having got out l.-b.-w. to Grimmett. Lancashire and Yorkshire added 96 for the 8th wicket making our 30 for four wickets look very small beside 324 for 8.· Both played grandly. Verity had a bit of luck but was worth all his 45, and Paynter's first Test innings of 77 was full of good strokes. He quite finished Grimmett's pretensions to appear in any more Tests of this tour. So we totalled 341, a save which gives a bowler a chance. And it proved so.

Again we got a good start, the Australians once more showing that however capable they are against plain medium pace up-and-down stuff they have no use for fast bowling, whoever bowls it.

At 1, 18, 34 and 51 we had Fingleton, Bradman, McCabe and Woodfull out, and barring a come-back by Ponsford, and Richardson coming off on his home wicket, we were sure to finish with a good first innings lead. Fortunately for Australia Ponsford came back all right, but there had been just a bare chance that Hammond would catch him for 3 in the slips. Only a Hammond could have got to that ball, but it nearly stuck!

Ponsford and Vic Richardson put on 80 for the fifth, Ponsford and Oldfield 63 more for the sixth and I was dreadfully sorry that Oldfield's innings should end as it did.

I bowled a ball *on the wicket*. Oldfield moved across *into the line of the ball* to hit it to leg. He struck too soon, and, in swinging his face round towards leg to avoid the ball, did not move it quickly enough. He was hit on the right side of his forehead, and directly I ran up to sympathise he said at once it was not my fault. Throughout Australia, with scarcely an exception, I got all the blame for this injury. I should say here that this happened on the third day.

Oldfield hit on the head

It was on the second that Woodfull, moving forward towards the off and *into the line* of the ball *which was a straight one*, missed it, and was hit over the heart. It was after this blow that he thought fit to inform the world that there were two sides playing and at one of them was not playing Cricket.

If that was not a definite charge of bad sportsmanship against the whole of the English XI then words do not really mean what they are generally supposed to mean. Afterwards, as the world knows, the famous Board of Control cable to M.C.C. said that Body-Line bowling is unsportsmanlike.

Having cabled that in January it was strange, to say the least of it, that next month the Board should cable "we do not regard the sportsmanship of your team as being in question." The two cables do not fit each other at all.

In January certain bowling which is used by the Captain, and strongly supported by the fielding of the whole team, is "unsportsmanlike." In February, though that bowling is still being used, the Captain using it and the team supporting it has sportsmanship which is "not the question"!

In April the Board passes a fatuous new Law, for use in Australia only (thank goodness!) and asks M.C.C. to make it a Law of the game. The new Law is aimed to prevent bowling "with intent to injure, &c., &c.," and was obviously framed to stop bowling which, in January, was officially called "unsportsmanlike." The Board of Control in Australia would seem to me to be playing at: "He loves me, he loves me not." Their cables have blown hot and cold between January and April, conveying an impression, which may prove to be the fact, that they don't understand what they are cabling about! Perhaps the senders of those conflicting cables can explain them. Nobody I have met in England is able to do so. To return to the Test. I have omitted to say that once more Ponsford was bowled behind his legs, walking too far across. Once the sixth wicket partnership was broken we finished off the innings for 222 and had thus secured a smashing lead of 119, which, failing a big innings by one or possibly two batsmen meant the match.

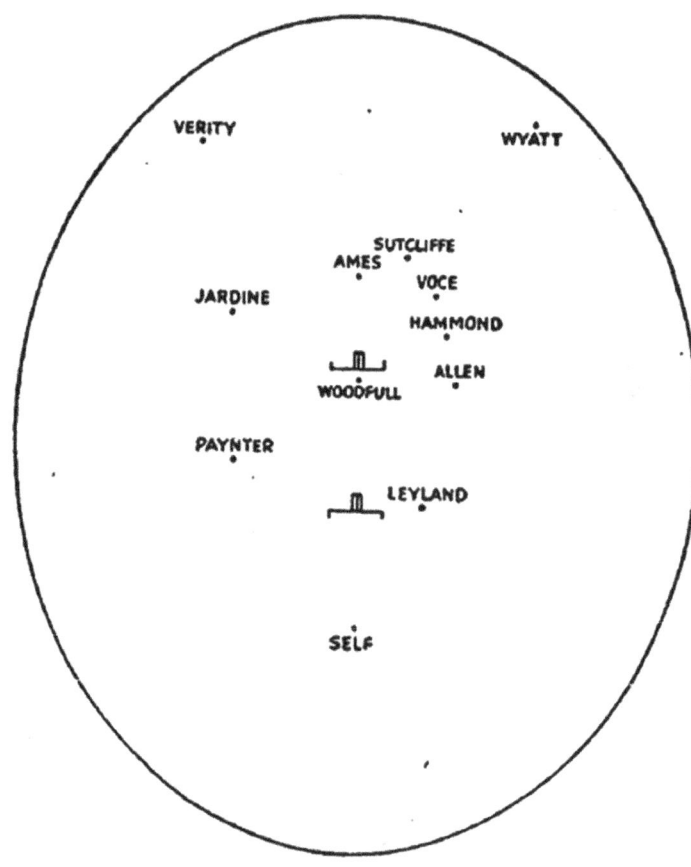

MY FIELD FOR WOODFULL.
Mr. Jardine sometimes between Mr. Allen and Hammond.

Our disappointment was keen when Sutcliffe chanced not to come off for the second time in the match, and was out at 7. He was out hooking. But Mr. Wyatt soon made amends, and with our Captain was not out at close of play with 85 up for one wicket, or a lead of 204 with 9 wickets in hand.

The fourth day was a pretty hot one, and we kept the Australians out in it from start to finish. Our first four individual scores were Mr. Jardine 56, Mr. Wyatt 42, Hammond 85 and Leyland 42. Good solid back-breaking stuff for the bowlers, even though no batsmen made three figures. Thus, at the end of that day we were 296 for 6, with Ames not out, but Paynter having a badly swollen ankle through running into a fence, was unlikely to be at his best next day. So it proved, and he made only one not out. But, so well did Verity bat once more that he and Ames were still there at lunch and we were 404 ahead with four wickets in hand.

This was virtually two in hand as Voce had a bad ankle and, with Paynter, was practically a passenger. Thus in the end we led Australia by 531 although we had batted to all intents and purposes two short.

Therefore, when we rattled out four of our opponents for 120, and they had Oldfield crocked, the game was practically ended on the fifth day after tea.

Next day both Woodfull and Bradman proved for everybody *who was watching the ·match and who can read the signs of cricket* that my Fast-Leg-Theory is not dangerous to the batsman or to his wicket. Again I tried my hardest but I got the wickets of only O'Reilly and Richardson, while Bradman made a brilliant 66 and Woodfull carried his bat right through an innings of this unsportsmanlike and physically dangerous stuff of mine for 73!!!

Is any further proof than such innings as these two *really* needed to show what utter nonsense the anti-Fast-Leg-Theory brigade are talking and writing?

In the end we won by 338 runs, and we should have won this game and others whether I had bowled Fast-Leg-Theory or not. I got 7 for 126 out of the 18 wickets that fell for 389 runs. Mr. Allen, who did not bowl LegTheory, took 8 for 121, and the remaining three fell, one each to Hammond, Voce, and Verity. It was not a Fast-Leg-Theory, much less a Body-Line, victory.

It was won because Australia's batsmen cannot play fast bowling that pitches on the wicket and off it on the leg side, instead of, futilely, wide on the off-side.

The sooner Australian Cricket recognises that fact the better for its own reputation for sportsmanlike behaviour, and for being able to give credit to its victors.

Scores follow overleaf.

ANGRY TEST SCENE WHEN OLDFIELD LAID OUT BY BALL

STRUCK ON HEAD BY FAST BALL FROM LARWOOD

Taken Away in Ambulance: Has Concussion

FRENZIED HOOTS BY CROWD

(By Hugh Buggy, "The News" Special Cricket Writer)

One of the wildest demonstrations ever seen on a cricket or football field took place on the Adelaide Oval today when Oldfield, the plucky little Australian wicketkeeper, was struck on the head with a fast ball from Larwood, the English express bowler, and immediately collapsed.

Oldfield, who was making a gallant stand for Australia, fell to the ground. A brave and fair reply was brought out and his head bathed as he lay on the green. After a while he managed to get to his feet and, with the assistance of Woodfull, staggered off the ground.

Meanwhile, the crowd, remembering Woodfull's protest against shock tactics only on Saturday, worked itself into a frenzy of indignation. The sense that followed has rarely been equalled before. Wild booming burst out in the outer ground, and the angry demonstrations were spread to the stands. Repeatedly the English bowler and fielders were severely jeered.

Anticipating trouble among police officers were hastily rushed to the oval. More men held in reserve at headquarters awaiting developments.

Oldfield was examined at the oval by Dr. C. F. Dolling and when a short time later he was taken away to be examined by Dr. Steele's team at Glenelg, he is suffering from slight concussion of the brain, accompanied by shock. It is thought that he may be able to play tomorrow.

"Ball Did Not Hit The Bat First"

[article columns of text]

Oldfield in Bad Way

[article columns of text]

Before the Tragedy

[article columns of text]

NO APOLOGY BY WOODFULL

Denies Statement by Mr. Warner

THREE HURT IN CITY BOUT

Trolly Hits Tram Standard

RUSTY NAIL IN BATON

Alleged Attack on Woman

"NEWS" SCOREBOARD

ENGLAND
First innings ... 341
Second innings ...

AUSTRALIA
First Innings
[scorecard]

OPIUM DEN DID GIRL'S STORY

"Woman There Smoking Pipe"

CHINESE FINED

HINKLER HIT ALPS?

Tourist Says He Saw Plane

CAPT. HOPE NOW SEARCHING

SWISS WILL AID

PILOT SCOPED TO FIND HINKLER ALIVE

POLICE INVESTIGATE GIRL'S DEATH

A Statement of Fact!

Although the year 1932 proved to be the most successful year in our history, we have every indication that it will be surpassed in 1933.

The Maintenance of Style, Quality, and Value

[advertisement text]

(4/4/- to 29/9/-)

Ingerson Ltd.

Third Test

ENGLAND

First Innings		Second Innings	
Sutcliffe, c. Wall, b. O'Reilly	9	c. sub. (O'Brien), b. Wall	7
D. R. Jardine, b. Wall	3	l.-b.-w., b. Ironmonger	56
Hammond, c. Oldfield, b. Wall	2	b. Bradman	85
Ames, b. Ironmonger	3	b. O'Reilly	69
Leyland, b. O'Reilly	83	c. Wall, b. Ironmonger	42
R. E. S. Wyatt, c. Richardson, b. Grimmett	78	c. Wall, b. O'Reilly	49
Paynter, c. Fingleton, b. Wall	77	not out	1
G. O. Allen, l.-b.-w., b. Grimmett	15	l.-b.-w., b. Grimmett	15
Verity, c. Richardson, b. Wall	45	l.-b.-w., b. O'Reilly	40
Voce, b. Wall	8	b. O'Reilly	8
Larwood, not out	3	c. Bradman, b. Ironmonger	8
Bye, 1; l.-b., 7; n.-b., 7	15	Byes, 17; l.-b., 11; n.-b., 4	32
Total	341	Total	412

FALL OF WICKETS

First Innings

1	2	3	4	5	6	7	8	9	10
4	16	16	30	186	196	228	324	336	341

Second Innings

1	2	3	4	5	6	7	8	9	10
7	91	123	154	245	296	394	395	400	412

BOWLING ANALYSIS

First Innings

	O.	M.	R.	W.		O.	M.	R.	W.
Wall	34.1	10	72	5	Grimmett	28	6	94	2
O'Reilly	50	19	82	2	McCabe	14	3	28	0
Ironmonger	20	6	50	1					

Second Innings

	O.	M.	R.	W.		O.	M.	R.	W.
Wall	29	6	75	1	Grimmett	35	9	74	1
O'Reilly	50.3	21	79	4	McCable	16	0	42	0
Ironmonger	57	21	87	3	Bradman	4	0	23	1

AUSTRALIA

First Innings		Second Innings	
W. M. Woodfull, b. Allen	22	not out	73
J. Fingleton, c. Ames, b. Allen	0	b. Larwood	0
D. G. Bradman, c. Allen, b. Larwood	8	c. and b. Verity	66
S. McCabe, c. Jardine, b. Larwood	8	c. Leyland, b. Allen	7
W. H. Ponsford, b. Voce	85	c. Jardine, b. Larwood	3
V. Y. Richardson, b. Allen	28	c. Allen, b. Larwood	21
W. A. Oldfield, retired hurt	41	absent hurt	—
C. V. Grimmett, c. Voce, b. Allen	10	b. Allen	6
T. W. Wall, b. Hammond	6	b. Allen	0
W. J. O'Reilly, b. Larwood	0	b. Larwood	5
H. Ironmonger, not out	0	b. Allen	0
Byes, 2; l.-b., 11; n.-b., 1	14	Byes, 4; l.-b., 2; n.-b., 5; 2., 1	12
Total	222	Total	193

FALL OF WICKETS
First Innings

1	2	3	4	5	6	7	8	9
1	18	34	51	131	194	212	222	222

Second Innings

1	2	3	4	5	6	7	8	9
3	12	100	116	171	183	183	192	193

BOWLING ANALYSIS
First Innings

	O.	M.	R.	W.		O.	M.	R.	W.
Larwood	25	6	55	3	Voce	14	5	21	1
Allen	23	4	71	4	Verity	16	7	31	0
Hammond	17.4	4	30	1					

Second Innings

	O.	M.	R.	W.		O.	M.	R.	W.
Larwood	19	3	71	4	Hammond	9	3	27	0
Allen	17.2	5	50	4	Verity	20	12	26	1
Voce	4	1	7	0					

At the conclusion of the third Test the averages were as follows.

England

BATTING

	Innings	Runs	Highest score	Times not out	Aver.
Paynter	2	78	77	1	78.00
Sutcliffe	6	296	194	1	59.20
Hammond	5	230	112	0	46.00
The Nawab of Pataudi	3	122	102	0	40.66
R. E. S. Wyatt	6	203	78	1	40.60
Leyland	5	166	83	0	33.20
Verity	3	87	45	0	29.00
G. O. Allen	5	102	30	0	20.40
D. R. Jardine	5	87	56	0	17.40
Ames	5	78	69	0	15.60
Larwood	5	24	9	1	6.00
Voce	5	22	8	1	5.50
Bowes	2	4	4*	2	4.00

BOWLING

	Overs	Maidens	Runs	Wickets	Aver.
Larwood	128.3	21	352	21	16.76
G. O. Allen	93.2	19	284	13	21.84
Hammond	76.5	18	170	7	24.28
Voce	99.3	20	293	12	24.41
Bowes	23	2	70	1	70.00
Verity	53	24	107	1	107.00

Australia

BATTING

	Innings	Runs	Highest score	Times not out	Aver.
D. G. Bradman	4	177	103*	1	59·00
S. J. McCabe	6	266	187*	1	53·20
W. H. Ponsford	4	122	85	0	30·50
V. Y. Richardson	6	164	49	0	27·33
W. M. Woodfull	6	138	73*	1	27·60
W. A. Oldfield	5	79	41*	2	26·33
F. J. Fingleton	6	150	83	0	25·00
L. Nagel	2	21	21*	1	21·00
A. F. Kippax	2	27	19	0	13·50
L. P. O'Brien	2	21	11	0	10·50
C. V. Grimmett	6	42	19	0	7·00
T. W. Wall	6	34	20	0	5·66
W. J. O'Reilly	6	31	15	0	5·16
H. Ironmonger	4	4	4	1	1·33

* Not out.

BOWLING

	Overs	Maidens	Runs	Wickets	Aver.
W. J. O'Reilly	226	94	407	19	21·42
D. G. Bradman	4	0	23	1	23·00
T. W. Wall	130·1	26	326	14	23·14
H. Ironmonger	110·1	39	191	8	23·87
L. Nagel	43·4	9	110	2	55·00
C. V. Grimmett	147	41	326	5	65·20
S. J. McCabe	45·1	5	113	1	113·00
A. F. Kippax	2	1	3	0	—

CHAPTER VIII

The Fourth Test

THE ASHES REGAINED – ENGLAND WINS AT THE LAST PLACE ON EARTH FIT FOR TEST CRICKET IN FEBRUARY – LANCASHIRE AND YORKSHIRE MUCH TO THE FORE – PAYNTER'S WARD-TO-WICKET CRICKET.

This will be known for all time as "Paynter's Match." I suggest that without his first innings display we should have lost it.

Mr. Jardine having run into something like his true form in the second innings of the third Test when going in first with Sutcliffe it was felt that now we had a settled first pair of batsmen. That knowledge is always calculated to inspire a side with a greater measure of confidence than it can ever have when its first pair is in doubt. So we got together on the eve of the fourth Test rather sure that the fate of the Ashes would be decided in this game and not at Sydney.

"Tangy" Voce had not been too fit so was left out, rightly I think, and Mitchell was included.

The game provided something of a triumph for our Yorkshire and Lancashire batsmen, their contributions to our success reading, Leyland 98, Paynter 97 for once out and Sutcliffe 88, which is very good indeed. Each played an innings of over 80, and the 83 of Paynter in the first innings was really a most courageous performance. Brisbane, if it has shortcomings in regard to the way the mercury bubbles up in its thermometers, has the great compensation of possessing one of the best "gates" in Australia. They cheered our little Lancashire lad almost – not quite – as though Bradman had made that 83.

Paynter had been taken pretty bad with tonsilitis, and after the first day's play was bundled off to hospital. We seemed sure to bat one short when news was received that Paynter was "on his way." Nobody could have looked less like runs than Eddie. At no time a great talker he had less than ever to say before he went in, and his naturally modest nature acted as such a brake when he came out at the end of his innings that a stranger, seeing him then for the first time, would never have guessed that he had just played a match-winning innings in the most important game of the rubber.

The Australians had made 340 and our score was 216 for 6 when

Paynter went in. There remained Verity, Mitchell and myself to bat. Paynter was ninth out at 356, a very fine performance indeed, even for a man who was fully fit. In Paynter's case I must say it was one of the most courageous I have ever seen played by anyone going in in the second half of the list. He had a temperature and his throat was bothering him a lot. Thus handicapped he proved that his fine innings at Adelaide in the third Test was not a fluke, also that he has the right temperament. for Test, or any kind of fighting cricket. Paynter had made lots of friends in Australia before he played in a Test. He increased their numbers considerably by his play when opportunity came. As, whenever he plays, Paynter has no superior as a field in whatever side he plays for, and indeed very few equals, he is one of England's greatest assets in my opinion. Stern critics can easily fault his batting if they want to do so, but to my mind it is the runs in the book that count, and not the words in the pavilion. There is always faultless batting and tall scoring!

Australia won the toss, and for the first time on this tour put up over a hundred for the first wicket. This was partly due to Woodfull taking Vic Richardson in with him. Whether he fails or not going in first is Vic's best place, as if he happens to come off he charges the bowlers much more heavily than would any of the others of the present Australian side.

Mr. Jardine rang his changes and shifted the field about, but the first pair seemed immovable and Richardson certain of his hundred when he was smartly stumped off Wally Hammond at 133.

I am inclined to the opinion that really we missed Voce in this match. Even if he is not getting wickets his bowling is so utterly different from that of all the others that he has an unsettling effect. But this is purely a matter of opinion, which is not due to the fact that Voce is a Notts. man, and I may be wrong.

Bradman came in at a time well suited for him. The shine was off the ball and he ·could have about an hour and a half's batting before we could call for a new ball. He played well from the start, trying no tricks at the beginning of his innings, and with 71 not out at the end of the day there is no doubt that he had much the better of the deal when stumps were drawn. Richardson 83, Woodfull 67, and McCabe 20 were the three men out, and, once again I ask, where is the intimidation, the unfairness, or the "not cricket" character in Fast-LegTheory bowling in the face of such a score as 251 for 3 on what, though a good wicket, is certainly not one of the world's best wickets?

I tried my absolute hardest and bowled as fast as I possibly could whenever I was put on, both for England and selfishly; because I had taken so far 21 wickets in this rubber when the fourth Test began, and I had four innings left in which to beat the previous bests in a rubber in Test cricket in Australia, viz: Maurice Tate's 38, and Arthur Mailey's 36. I had to take 18 wickets out of a possible 40 to do it, a tall order but not impossible, considering that I was. quit fit, Australia a bit rattled, and the last two innings were to be played at Sydney where, in the first Test, I had taken ten wickets.

Richardson strokes Larwood to square leg in the 4th Test, Brisbane.

But no matter how I tried I could not get a wicket that day. I am very glad to say nobody was struck, 251 runs were scored and yet the general complaint against Fast-Leg-Theory is as fresh now as it was during the height of the rumpus at Adelaide. The attitude of the Antis is really very inconsistent. If batsmen get hit there's a row, if they don't get hit there is no withdrawal of the row, only more serious endeavour by appointing a special committee for the express purpose of legislating this "terror" out of the game.

What a farce it all is, and, as Noble wrote about the allegations that I bowl "at" my man, what humbug.

On the second day at Brisbane I got on the move again knocking Bradman's off stump out of its original position after he had made only five more runs, and, helped by Ponsford's advance towards point to play a straight leg stump ball, treating his leg peg similarly three runs later. So that from 251 for 3, and Bradman in possession, we jumped to 267 for 5 and both he and Ponsford out.

I reckon that was the best half hour I put in on this last tour; for it has to be clearly understood that with fourth innings to play we could scarcely have won that most important Test had these two players really dug in with such a score as 251 for 3 as their foundation.

Bradman helped matters by attempting a very flashy stroke at once. He tried to cut a straight ball of fairly good length. It's a brilliant success when bat and ball connect, but the limit of unsound batting when they don't.

From the fall of the fifth wicket at 267 we got wickets at regular intervals, so that from 251 and only 3 out Australia had the disappointing total of 340.

Thus we took 7 for 89 that day in a sweltering heat, and that was probably the best all round performance our bowling and fielding achieved on this tour.

Mr. Jardine and Sutcliffe, playing stubbornly on the moral effect which this small score had on the Australians, went in and stayed in until the umpires removed the bails. They were not idle either, as they made 99 runs, which was good to be going on with on the Monday. Mr. Jardine was first out at 114, mis-timing O'Reilly, and Hammond helped Sutcliffe to add 43 before McCabe bowled him at 157 for 2. Then our opponents got us well "on the run," no wicket adding more than 25 runs until Paynter and I put on 39 for the 8th wicket.

Then Verity and Paynter almost repeated their 8th wicket stand of 96 in the third Test by adding 92 for the 9th wicket, passing Australia's total in doing so. That was a grand partnership, Verity's batting strongly supporting the few good judges who had hinted at his batting ability some time ago.

We led by 16 runs and really soon had the match won directly we got the first wicket at 46, by getting the next three, including Bradman, Richardson and Ponsford at 79, 81 and 91. It would be an exaggeration to say we feared that the tail would waggle, but we did not like the look of the sky with the possibility of having to get over 100 against O'Reilly and Ironmonger on a sticky dog in the fourth innings.

That our position was an anxious one is shown by the fact that with 6 wickets standing Australia had a lead of 92 runs, the wicket had definitely worn and rain was "about."

Next day we had a stroke of luck when Love ran out Darling for us. Darling had made a good 39 and was looking threatening when this happened. Largely owing to this mishap their last five men made only 16 runs and we were left with 160 to get.

This, it will always seem to me was a fine all-round performance by England once Australia had made 251 for 3 on the first day. Yes, I think England took the honours in this game.

But not so without a shiver or two in the second innings. Thus

Sutcliffe got a touch and Darling held the snick off Tim Wall with only 5 runs made. Our Captain had ordered Leyland in if a wicket fell quickly and splendidly did Maurice do his job. He was not out 66 at close of play, Mr. Jardine, with only 24, having stopped up one end completely until, with 78 scored, he was out l.-b.-w. to Ironmonger. We had 107 for 2 when bad light, which made rain more probable, stopped play. Fortunately, the rain held off and next day Maurice added 20 more runs and with Paynter clinching "his" match with a six we were home.

I must not omit to mention Woodfull's sporting attention to Paynter in this game. The Australian captain performed all those little courtesies which mean so much, and which in the present instance went far to soothe ruffled feelings.

Spectators were allowed in at half price on the last day and the gate totalled £9,741. This compares, of course, unfavourably with the takings at the three chief centres in Australia but is fairly good for Brisbane where, however, for climatic reasons there should never be again a Test match in late February.

Sir Leslie Wilson, the Governor of Queensland, presided at a final reception given by the Queensland Cricket Association, which was attended by both teams.

Mr. D. R. Jardine declared that it was a great match, but that probably the greatest Test in history was the second Test Match at Melbourne, when Australia won.

"I am naturally delighted," he said, "that we have regained the Ashes, but I hope I can say with Kipling that cricketers can meet triumph and disaster and treat the two impostors in just the same way."

W. M. Woodfull, the Australian captain, congratulated us and said· he hoped that in 1934 the Australians would repeat their 1930 performance when they won the Ashes. "Our defeat will only spur us on to do a little better next time," he said.

Mr. Jardine also made the following statement to Renter's correspondent: "I have been thrice lucky in the side which it has been my proud privilege to lead. No captain has received or could ask for greater help, sympathy, and utter loyalty than has fallen to my lot. We are proud of our success against gallant and determined opponents. We condole with them on the sad loss of Archie Jackson."

Referring to the host of letters of good will that he had received from Australians, Mr. Jardine said that these correspondents appreciated silence instead of comment and criticism on matters of controversy from visitors and guests.

"They echo the hope that the game of cricket is all that matters," said he, "and the best and only thing to do is to get on with it, for there is little if anything wrong with it."

Sentiments with which every English cricketer, and I do not doubt most Australian cricketers as well, entirely agree.

Fourth Test

AUSTRALIA

First Innings		Second Innings	
V. Y. Richardson st. Ames b. Hammond	83	c. Jardine b. Verity	32
W. M. Woodfull b. Mitchell	67	c. Hammond b. Mitchell	19
D. G. Bradman b. Larwood	76	c. Mitchell b. Larwood	24
S. J. McCabe c. Jardine b. Allen	20	b. Verity	22
W. H. Ponsford b. Larwood	19	c. Larwood b. Allen	0
L. Darling c. Ames b. Allen	17	run out	39
E. H. Bromley c. Verity b. Larwood	26	c. Hammond b. Allen	7
H. S. Love l.-b.-w., b. Mitchell	5	l.-b.-w., b. Larwood	3
T. Wall, not out	6	c. Jardine, b. Allen	2
W. J. O'Reilly, c. Hammond, b. Larwood	6	b. Larwood	4
H. Ironmonger, st. Ames, b. Hammond	8	not out	0
Byes, 5; l.-b., 1; n.-b., 1	7	Byes, 13; l.b., 9; n.-b., 1	23
Total	340	Total	175

FALL OF WICKETS
First Innings

1	2	3	4	5	6	7	8	9	10
133	200	233	264	267	292	315	317	329	340

Second Innings

1	2	3	4	5	6	7	8	9	10
46	79	81	91	136	163	169	169	171	175

BOWLING ANALYSIS
First Innings

	O.	M.	R.	W.		O.	M.	R.	W.
Larwood	31	7	101	4	Mitchell	16	5	49	2
Allen	24	4	83	2	Verity	27	12	39	0
Hammond	23	5	61	2					

Second Innings

	O.	M.	R.	W.		O.	M.	R.	W.
Larwood	17.3	3	49	3	Verity	19	6	30	2
Allen	17	3	44	3	Mitchell	5	0	11	1
Hammond	10	4	18	0					

ENGLAND

First Innings		Second Innings	
D. R. Jardine, c. Love, b. O'Reilly	46	l.-b.-w., b. Ironmonger	24
Sutcliffe, l.-b.-w., b. O'Reilly	86	c. Darling, b. Wall	2
Hammond, b. McCabe	20	c. Bromley, b. Ironmonger	14
R. E. S. Wyatt, c. Love, b. Ironmonger	12		
Leyland, c. Bradman, b. O'Reilly	12	c. McCabe, b. O'Reilly	86
Ames, c. Darling, b. Ironmonger	17	not out	14
G. O. Allen, c. Love, b. Wall	13		
Paynter, c. Richardson, b. Ironmonger	83	not out	14
Larwood, b. McCabe	23		
Verity, not out	23		
Mitchell, l.-b.-w., b. O'Reilly	0		
Byes, 6; l.-b., 12; n.-b., 3	21	Byes, 2; l.-b., 4; n.-b., 2; w., 1	9
Total	356	Total (4 wkts.)	163

FALL OF WICKETS

First Innings

1	2	3	4	5	6	7	8	9	10
114	157	165	188	198	216	225	264	356	356

Second Innings

1	2	3	4
5	78	118	138

BOWLING ANALYSIS

First Innings

	O.	M.	R.	W.		O.	M.	R.	W.
Wall	33	6	66	1	Bromley	10	4	19	0
O'Reilly	67.4	26	120	4	Bradman	7	1	17	0
Ironmonger	43	19	69	3	Darling	2	0	4	0
McCabe	23	7	40	2					

Second Innings

	O.	M.	R.	W.		O.	M.	R.	W.
Wall	7	1	17	1	Ironmonger	35	13	47	2
O'Reilly	30	11	65	1	McCabe	7.4	2	25	0

McCabe hits Larwood to the boundary, 4th Test.

CHAPTER IX

The Fifth Test

WE DROP SOME DIFFICULT CATCHES – DON TRIES TO HIT ME TO THE OFF – AWKWARD FACTS FOR AUSTRALIA'S BOARD OF CONTROL! – ALEXANDER'S FOOTMARKS – MR. WYATT AGAIN BATS WELL – HAMMOND'S BIG HIT – HE ENDS A FIERY RUBBER WITH A CRASHING SIX!

Woodfull won the toss again, this being the fourth time in this series that he did so, and we trooped out to confront the "Hill" once more; this time with Voce for Mitchell as the only change from the side that won at Brisbane.

We got off the mark well, as Mr. Jardine made a good catch in the slips to get rid of Vic Richardson who thus became a "candidate," and was duly elected in the second innings! I was really sorry to see such a popular man "bag 'em," but it's all in the game, and if Richardson is in England next season no doubt he will get his own back with interest.

Early on in this innings I had hopes of beating the individual record for wickets taken in the Tests in one season in Australia, as I soon had three wickets for only 14 runs, and those three were Richardson, Woodfull and Bradman.

From a glance at the score the reader will wonder how, since Bradman made 48, I managed to get 3 for 14 when he was out. This was done owing to Mr. Jardine's frequent changes of bowling, as Bradman managed to get most of his runs when I was not bowling. In this innings he made some spasmodic attempts to hit me on the off but not always successfully.

"Tangy" Voce, who is usually such a good field, put two possible chances on the carpet when O'Brien was in the thirties and forties, otherwise there would have been no partnership, as there was, of 99 by him and McCabe for the fourth wicket.

Darling, who eventually made 83, began none too well. He was missed, a not too easy catch and bowl chance by Allen, when he had made 12 and Herbert Sutcliffe had made a very good attempt to catch him a run earlier. But after this Darling did not look back, doing most of the scoring in the 81 put on for the fifth wicket with McCabe, who was then bowled by Verity for a good 73, which had begun some time since to look very dangerous for us. Oldfield soon dug in and was with Darling, then

66 not out, when we left the field.

The "Hill" had been fairly quiet all day, which was in accordance with their usual behaviour when Australia is doing fairly well. Proving once more that the main cause of their outbreaks is their own ingrained inability to take a licking.

Clem Hill says they are the best judges of cricket in the world. If that is so, it is remarkable that they who cursed when I bowled Leg-Theory with three or four short-legs in other Tests did not applaud when, in this Test, I bowled frequently with four shortslips. Perhaps their rage with me had so blinded them that they did not notice this different setting of the field!

Next day Bill Oldfield got his ears back, and had been actually over 2½ hours at the wicket before he was splendidly thrown out by Eddie Paynter. That was a jolly good thing for us, because after Verity, round the wicket, had bowled Darling at 328 : 6 : 83 Lee had come in and, tapping me into the outfield, was looking like staying. As it was, after Oldfield's run out at 385 for 7 the last 3 wickets added 50 runs.

It was a fine solid performance on Australia's part. Their innings containing as it did six scores of over 40 and three over 60 was but one more positive proof that the howling against Leg-Theory was just so much nonsense. Although I and Voce both bowled with slip-fields in this, as in other Test innings, we both bowled also with the full complement of leg-side fielders as we had before. There was no kind of relaxation of effort on my part.

Yet, a glance at the result shows that Australia batted *for the whole of one day, and a good part of the second,* for a total of 435 runs on the fastest wicket there is in Australia to-day (therefore, presumably specially suitable for results with very fast bowling if aimed "at" the batsman), without a batsman getting hurt, scarcely one ever getting hit, and a total absence of that "intensely bitter feeling between the players as well as injury" which the Australian Board of Control thought fit to broadcast to the world, entirely disregardless of the feelings of their visitors, and, I may add, the Truth.

If the members of that Board were watching this match, and if they understand the game of cricket, they must have been furious that no Australian batsman was injured. For they must have seen the actual play making their unfortunate cable looking more and more foolish as the Australian innings went on without any kind of casualty! It was really rather bad luck for them, but I can assure them, whether they believe it or not, that I bowled at Sydney exactly as I had in every other innings of this tour, and, except for the natural staleness at the end of a tour, much of

Ames run out in the 5th Test.
Woodfull bowled Larwood in the 5th Test.

which had not been by way of a rest cure, every bit as fast as I could.

I can only suggest again that if the Australian Board of Control was present at this innings, and if it understands cricket, that the end of the innings was the time for it *to abandon all idea of going on with its Special Committee*, which, in the end, has succeeded only in making itself look foolish in the eyes of the cricket world, and not all of that outside Australia either, by giving to posterity the "ThoughtReader." The Australian Board might at least have saved Messrs. Hartigan, Noble, Woodfull and Richardson from perpetrating that absurd blunder.

In this innings some of us managed to put some takeable catches on the carpet, but as the catching had been fairly sound throughout the rubber as a whole, this lapse may be excused.

When we went in Mr. Jardine could not get going, but thanks to a very fine partnership by Hammond, at his best, and Sutcliffe, of 122 for the second wicket we had 159 on the book for two out at the end of the second day.

I must state here that when our innings began, after England had bowled 108.2 overs, there were no boot marks near enough to the line of the wicket to be of any use to any bowler. Therefore what happened afterwards *was not due to any English bowler*, and least of all to Mr. Allen, who had been so unfairly accused before the first Test at Sydney by M. A. Noble and W. W. Armstrong of cutting up the wicket. I was sent in overnight and was 5 not out when we resumed on the third day. The second wicket had fallen at 153. When Hammond was out at 245 : 2 : 101, he being the only batsman to make a couple of centuries in this series, he and I had added 92 runs and he had been batting for over three hours. I have seen Leyland bat better than he did in this innings, but somehow I seemed to get most of the bowling, and, as some of it was not up to our county form in England, I did my best to help both the side and self. I got most of my runs forcing, but, as luck would have it, failed to hit properly the ball that mattered most! I had just made 14 off four balls from Lee, who was bowling off-turners that did not always bend much, and mishit the fifth, lobbing up a catch to mid-on. Of course, it happened to be caught by Ironmonger, who is not the best fielder who has appeared in Test cricket, and my wonderful chance of scoring a century in a Test match had gone. I made my 98 in just about two hours and a quarter, and, going in at 153 for 2, was out at 310 : 4 : 98.

Twenty runs later Leyland was run out, and at close of play, Mr. Wyatt having made a careful 51, Mr. Allen was not out 25.

On the fourth day he made 23 more and when Bradman made a fine catch to dismiss him our innings was over with a lead of 19 runs.

This innings, on top of our magnificent win in the fourth Test after Australia had made such a strong start in the first innings of it, proved quite conclusively that whether our tactics in the field were unsportsmanlike or not, our batting was too good for their bowling. Even the Australian Press, the Australian Board of Control and their Special Committee cannot frame a law to prevent *that* fact going down to posterity.

In Australia's second innings they made another bad start, Vic Richardson playing my second ball into Mr. Allen's hands at short-leg, the first wicket falling before a run had been scored. Bradman very soon "saw" the ball and made some really magnificent strokes. He again tried to get runs off me on the off-side, but again found that fast-legstump bowling, pitching a good length, or just short of it, cannot often be hit in that direction.

I was beginning to have serious trouble in the ball of my left foot before my innings was over. This became so painful early in Australia's second innings that I had to leave the field about three-thirty, and did not bowl again in the innings. I ask the reader to note well those two facts.

Verity soon found that Alexander's follow-up had made marks just where he might use them.

I do not remember reading anything from the pens and brains of Messrs. Noble or Armstrong saying that Woodfull must expect a protest from Mr. Jardine if he, Woodfull, continued to bowl Alexander. Nor did either of those writers tell Woodfull in print that if either J. J. Darling or G. H. S. Trott had been captain they would not have put Alexander on to bowl.

No, that baseless accusation against Mr. Allen and that taunt at Mr. Jardine before the first Test, was made *because they are Englishmen.* That which Messrs. Allen and Jardine must not do may be done with impunity, and without adverse criticism, by W. M. Woodfull and H. H. Alexander, apparently because they are Australians.

It was rather amusing that Verity should get 5 for 33, making some use of the cut-up of an Australian bowler!

But perhaps Messrs. Noble and Armstrong, who had made such haste to practically criticise Mr. Allen out of the first Test, did not see the fifth Test.

It seems to me that before Mr. E. E. Bean; who has been Chairman of the Australian Board of Control, criticises me, as he did about May 8th last, for what he calls "offensive criticism," he should first stop the offensive criticism that went on near his own doorstep. Nothing I can write or say now can put any Australian player off his game, and not one word in this book is written in such a vain hope, but if Mr. Bean tells me that what Noble and Armstrong wrote before the first Test about Mr. Allen was not likely to upset him and cause him to bowl far below form then I must beg to differ from Mr. Bean.

On that fourth afternoon McCabe was not very well in himself, and with Verity grateful for Alexander's assistance Australia would have cut a sorry figure but for Woodfull and Bradman, who made 138 runs of the total of 175 from the bat.

I cannot refrain here from expressing the hope that the Australian Board of Control in full force were watching this Australian innings also. I have a very special reason for this, because what I am going to write knocks the bottom out of the flimsy case of the Australian Board of Control, if it ever had a case.

I am told, in different words it is true, by the Board, its Special Committee, and those portions of the Australian Press which has supported the "Thought-Reader," that I bowl with "intent to intimidate or to injure." If it is not at me, is it perhaps at Mitchell or Verity that the "Thought-Reader" is aimed? I assume, however, that I am the Culprit-inChief. Very well.

It follows naturally, therefore, that if my Fast-Leg-Theory is *not in action* all will be well in Cricket, and Australian committee men, Australian Pressmen, Australian Cricketers, and those infallible and sweet-voiced judges of the game, the Australian Barrackers, will have nothing to complain about.

Then, how comes it that the Australian innings in which I bowled *the fewest number of overs of the ten that I bowled in* (while I am off the field for the last ninety minutes' play) happens to be *the least productive innings but two* of Australia's ten innings and, *without the help of rain and sun, also one of their shortest?*

It seems to me that if the Australian Board of Control, and their Specialists and slavish followers in their Press, are talking and writing sense, then, when I am either bowling very few overs, or am not even on the field of play at all, Australian batsmen should be in clover. They should be hitting fours freely, without fear of the ambulance.

But no! I am wrong. Actually when my Fast-Leg-Theory is *not in action* Australian batsmen get out even more quickly than when it is!

For purposes of comparison I give here a table showing the number of overs I bowled, the wickets I took, and the Australian totals in each of the ten innings of this rubber.

	Overs.	Wickets.	Australian Score.
1	31	5	360
2	18	5	164
3	20	2	228
4	15	.2	191
5	25	3	222
6	19	4	193
7	31	4	340
8	17	3	175
9	32	4	435
10	11	1	182

A glance at this table shows that whenever I bowled most overs, and consequently whenever there was most of this dreadfully intimidating, injuring stuff, Australia made most runs!!!

The more I go into *the facts* of the tour the fewer do I find to agree with anything the Australian Board, or its Specialists, or its Press have *ever* said or written between them during this tour. It is a sad commentary. But perhaps I am prejudiced in my own favour.

We were left with 164 to get to win and the rest of 1933 to do it in.

Harold Larwood (left) on the way to his 98 at the SCG.

Between us and victory were only those footmarks which the eagle-eyed Noble and Armstrong had missed. There was nothing much of them but they were there all the same, and our friendly old enemy Ironmonger proceeded to hit them. The first time he did so to count, Mr. Jardine was out at 43. Ironmonger at once surprised Leyland by bringing one back off the "Alexander," to hit Maurice's pads and go on to the wicket, at the same total. But then Mr. Wyatt helped Hammond, who was again in great form, to take the score to 70 for two by lunch time. After the interval Wally saw it as big as, a balloon and hit the bowling all over the place.

One drive sent the ball along a passage and down some stairs into a bar, to interrupt a discussion on how to stop Body-Line. Which it seems to me is about the best place in which to discuss that nonsense endlessly.

Mr. Wyatt, too, was playing more freely than usual. Altogether it was a bright and convincing finish to the rubber. A rubber regarding which about the only contention which the Press of the beaten side, but certainly not of the beaten eleven, have appeared not to have made, is that the better side lost it.

Hammond rounded off this noisy series with a smashing sixer off O'Reilly, and all was definitely over-bar the shouting! Though we had already had some of that, too.

*****

The summing-up on these five Tests – the cricket side of them, ignoring all surrounding atmosphere – is not difficult. Therefore I will be brief.

The rubber was won by England, in spite of losing the toss four times in five, because of Australian incompetence against perfectly fair fast-bowling whatever its tactics.

Proof of this is there for all to see in the fact that, though Mr. Allen never bowled Fast-LegTheory with my setting of the field, he got 21 wickets all the same; five more wickets in five more balls bowled in the whole series than were taken by Tim Wall the Australian fast bowler. If, therefore, the Australians of 1932-33 were competent players of fast bowling which never uses Leg-Theory, Mr. Allen could not possibly have done so well.

I hold it to be so finally proved that, in the usual cricket phrase, "the Australians can't play fast bowling," that I do not hesitate to forecast now that even on our slower wickets we shall retain the Ashes next season – especially if it is a dry one – if the English eleven contains at least three fast bowlers fit and well.

For example, I should not fancy Australia's chance in any Test on a hard wicket next season against Voce, Clark of Northants and myself, if we were all fit and in form. I must not be understood to be suggesting here that we should be the three fast bowlers to the exclusion of any others, put merely mention these three by way of illustration.

It does not matter that at any rate one of the three would have to do some bowling after the ball had lost some of its shine. The Australians were not beaten this time by the new ball.

They were beaten, to write more accurately, very largely by a new application of the ball, which got them guessing all the time.

In the second place, their defeat was assisted by the weakness of their own bowling. Australia's sole bowling strength in the last two Tests actually consisted of only three bowlers, one of whom is getting on for fifty years of age, and one of whom, O'Reilly, though a class bowler, was showing signs of overbowling. O'Reilly bowled 153 more overs in the Tests than myself, and I bowled 49 more overs than any other Englishmen.

Australia had apparently no fresh bowling to throw into an already beaten attack by the time the fourth Test was reached. In my opinion that was bad selection. Because the bowlers were there, at hand. They should have included Tobin, or Lee, as a fourth bowler, in place of Bromley in the fourth Test.

It is not possible, without greater luck than Cricket ever gives, for three bowlers, one of whom is an old man in the Test cricket sense, to stand the strain of dealing successfully with a winning opponent in such a climate as Brisbane's. For that very vital Test the Australian selectors showed decidedly bad judgment of the situation. They recognised their mistake and amended it, when it was too late to retain the Ashes, by playing four bowlers in the fifth Test.

But a selection committee *of cricketers* would never have chosen the Australian XI which we beat at Brisbane. And it would never have left out Bradman from the first Test.

Apart from the risk of taking us on with only three bowlers they blundered badly also by including H. S. Love as wicket-keeper. He *was* a Test class wicket-keeper, but he is now 38, and is not so good as the young South Australian, C. W. Walker, who is only 24 and, in the opinion of many people, almost the equal of Bill Oldfield at his best.

In fielding there was not much, if anything, to choose between the two sides. Australia had no superior to Paynter, though Bradman is still a wonderfully good field, and they had no superior to my skipper at holding hot catches in positions near the wicket.

As a set of fielders, Messrs. Jardine, Allen and Wyatt with Paynter, Hammond and Voce can hold their own with any Australian six.

Ames proved himself little, if any, inferior to Bill Oldfield as a wicket-keeper.

Finally, we had certainly the better Captain. Reversing the positions of the two concerned I can only judge by Woodfull's extraordinary behaviour at Adelaide that he would have crumpled to nothing under the treatment my skipper received in Australia. I know nothing at all about the hysteria in the Australians' dressing room, but I do know that we of the England XI would have gone anywhere and done anything for our skipper. England's Eleven will be indeed fortunate if, in the future, it ever has to serve under a better man than Mr. Jardine.

Fifth Test

AUSTRALIA

	First Innings		Second Innings	
V. Y. Richardson, c. Jardine, b. Larwood	.. .. ..	0	c. Allen, b. Larwood ..	0
W. M. Woodfull, b. Larwood	..	14	b. Allen	67
D. G. Bradman, b. Larwood		48	b. Verity	71
L. P. O'Brien, c. Larwood, b. Voce		61	c. Verity, b. Voce ..	5
S. J. McCabe, c. Hammond, b. Verity	.. .. ..	73	c. Jardine, b. Voce ..	4
L. Darling, b. Verity	.. ..	85	c. Wyatt, b. Verity	7
W. A. Oldfield, run out	..	52	c. Wyatt, b. Verity..	5
P. K. Lee, c. Jardine, b. Verity		42	b. Allen	15
W. J. O'Reilly, b. Allen	..	19	b. Verity	1
H. H. Alexander, not out	..	17	l.-b.-w., b. Verity ..	0
H. Ironmonger, b. Larwood	..	1	not out	0
Byes, 13; l.-b., 9; w., 1 ..		23	Byes, 4; n.-b., 3 ..	7
Total	.. .. ..	435	Total	182

FALL OF WICKETS

First Innings

1	2	3	4	5	6	7	8	9	10
0	59	64	163	244	328	385	414	430	435

Second Innings

1	2	3	4	5	6	7	8	9	10
0	115	135	139	148	161	177	178	178	182

BOWLING ANALYSIS

First Innings

	O.	M.	R.	W.		O.	M.	R.	W.
Larwood ..	32·2	10	98	4	Verity ..	17	8	62	3
Voce ..	24	4	80	1	Hammond	8	0	32	0
Allen ..	25	1	128	1	Wyatt ..	2	0	12	0

Second Innings

	O.	M.	R.	W.		O.	M.	R.	W.
Larwood ..	11	0	44	1	Voce ..	10	0	34	2
Allen ..	11·4	2	54	2	Verity ..	19	9	33	5
Hammond	3	0	10	0					

ENGLAND

First Innings		Second Innings	
Sutcliffe, c. Richardson, b. O'Reilly	56		
D. R. Jardine, c. Oldfield, b. O'Reilly	18	c. Richardson, b. Ironmonger	24
Hammond, l.-b.-w., b. Lee	101	not out	75
Larwood, c. Ironmonger, b. Lee	98		
Leyland run out	42	b. Ironmonger	0
R. E. S. Wyatt, c. Ironmonger, b. O'Reilly	51	not out	61
Ames, run out	4		
Paynter, b. Lee	9		
G. O. Allen, c. Bradman, b. Lee	48		
Verity, c. Oldfield, b. Alexander	4		
Voce, not out	7		
Byes, 7; l.-b., 7; n.-b., 2	16	Byes, 6; l.-b., 1; n.-b., 1	8
Total	454	Total (2 wkts.)	168

FALL OF WICKETS

First Innings

1	2	3	4	5	6	7	8	9	10
31	153	245	310	330	349	374	418	434	454

Second Innings

1	2
43	43

BOWLING ANALYSIS

First Innings

	O.	M.	R.	W.		O.	M.	R.	W.
Alexander	35	1	129	1	Lee	40.2	11	111	4
McCabe	12	1	27	0	Darling	7	5	3	0
O'Reilly	45	7	100	3	Bradman	1	0	4	0
Ironmonger	31	13	64	0					

Second Innings

	O.	M.	R.	W.		O.	M.	R.	W.
Alexander	11	2	25	0	Lee	12.2	3	52	0
O'Reilly	15	5	32	0	McCabe	5	2	10	0
Ironmonger	26	12	34	2	Darling	2	0	7	0

The complete averages for the Test Matches are as follows:

Australia

BATTING

	Innings	Runs	Highest score	Times not out	Aver.
D. G. Bradman	8	396	103*	1	56.57
S. J. McCabe	10	385	187*	1	42.77
L. Darling	4	148	85	0	37.00
W. M. Woodfull	10	305	73*	1	36.11
P. K. Lee	2	57	42	0	28.50
V. Y. Richardson	10	279	83	0	27.90
W. A. Oldfield	7	136	52	2	27.20
F. J. Fingleton	6	150	83	0	25.00
W. H. Ponsford	6	141	85	0	23.50
L. P. O'Brien	4	87	61	0	21.75
L. Nagel	2	21	21*	1	21.00
H. H. Alexander	2	17	17*	1	17.00
E. H. Bromley	2	33	26	0	16.50
A. F. Kippax	2	27	19	0	13.50
C. V. Grimmett	6	42	19	0	7.00
W. J. O'Reilly	10	61	19	0	6.10
T. Wall	8	42	20	1	6.00
H. S. Love	2	8	5	0	4.00
H. Ironmonger	8	13	8	3	2.60

* not out.

BOWLING

	Overs	Maidens	Runs	Wickets	Aver.
T. Wall	170.1	33	409	16	25.56
W. J. O'Reilly	383.4	143	724	27	26.81
H. Ironmonger	245.1	96	405	15	27.00
P. K. Lee	52.4	14	163	4	40.75
D. G. Bradman	12	1	44	1	44.00
L. Nagel	43.4	9	110	2	55.00
C. V. Grimmett	147	41	326	5	65.20
S. J. McCabe	92.5	17	215	3	71.66
H. H. Alexander	46	3	154	1	154.00
L. Darling	11	5	14	0	—
E. H. Bromley	10	4	19	0	—
A. F. Kippax	2	1	3	0	—

England

BATTING

	Innings	Runs	Highest score	Times not out	Aver.
Paynter	5	184	83	2	61.33
Sutcliffe	9	440	194	1	55.00
Hammond	9	440	112	1	55.00
R. E. S. Wyatt	9	327	78	2	46.71
The Nawab of Pataudi	3	122	102	0	40.66
Leyland	9	306	86	0	34.00
Verity	5	114	45	1	28.50
Larwood	7	145	98	1	24.15
G. O. Allen	7	163	48	0	23.28
D. R. Jardine	9	199	56	0	22.11
Ames	8	113	69	1	16.14
Voce	6	29	8	2	7.25
Bowes	2	4	4*	2	—
Mitchell	1	0	0	0	—

* Not out.

BOWLING

	Overs	Maidens	Runs	Wickets	Aver.
Larwood	220·2	41	644	33	19·51
Mitchell	21	5	60	3	20·00
Verity	135	54	271	11	24·63
Voce	133·3	24	407	15	27·13
Allen	171	29	593	21	28·23
Hammond	120·5	27	291	9	32·33
Bowes	23	2	70	1	70·00
Wyatt	2	0	12	0	—

Bill Woodfull, the Australian skipper.

CHAPTER X

Australia Now – and To-morrow

Although England holds the Ashes it would be most unwise for anyone to form now the definite opinion that we shall still be in possession in mid-August, 1934.

A sense of that true patriotism which holds the enemy in due, but not undue, respect causes me to offer a note of warning against over-optimism even so early as almost a year before the Australian team of 1934 is chosen. That we had the better team on their wickets on the last tour I have not the slightest doubt. I believe that the bulk of sober and sound opinion among Australians themselves will agree with that view.

But their wickets are not our wickets, and the same two sets of players who fought December, 1932 to March, 1933, would very likely not have produced a 4 to 1 win for England on her own pitches.

73.1 per cent of the Australian wickets fell to fast bowling, counting Bill Voce as such and Hammond as medium paced, whereas, by way of comparison, in 1930, in England our fast bowlers took 35.5 per cent. of Australia's wickets. This vast difference in destructiveness between almost the same sets of bowlers against the same batsmen in 1930 and in 1932-33 can only be made good in 1934 if the same or equally good fast bowlers who took the 73 per cent. in Australia do so again; or if Australia's batting is weaker in 1934 than it was on the recent tour; or if England's slow and slow mediums are good enough to adjust the scales.

I saw enough in Australia on the recent tour to satisfy me that the difference in matchwinning power between the Australians and ourselves is just slight enough to promise that the next rubber is absolutely certain to be a very close thing unless one side has all the weather luck. That, as we all know, rarely happens, England's rain and sun to-day in England being Australia's to-morrow.

How true it is that the luck in cricket is very evenly shared, as between two old and very regular opponents, is proved by the fact that over the whole series of Tests we have won the toss 65 times to Australia's 64, while both sides have now won 51 matches each. Even the number of players who have made centuries in Test cricket shares absolutely this astonishing equality, both countries owning 38 each. England with 85 has scored 3 more centuries than Australia, and an almost even more surprising levelness is in the fact that while 712 Englishmen have been bowled 708 Australians have shared that fate. Australia with 264 has 29 more duck's eggs than we in her basket, and her men have been adjudged 1.-b.-w. 1,039 times to the 940 of England.

But Australia has two records which England ought to have, viz.:– the highest total, 729 for 6 wickets, declared (in 1930 at Lord's), against our 636; and the highest individual score, Bradman's 334 (at Leeds in 1930) to the late R. E. Foster's 287 (at Sydney in 1903). I hope it will be very long before either of these records is broken.

But Australia has also the lowest score, 36 (at Birmingham, in 1902, Rhodes, 7 for 17, Hirst, 3 for 15) against our 45 (at Sydney, in 1887, C. T. B. Turner, 6 for 15, and J. J. Ferris, 4 for 27) scored, I regret to say, with six Notts. men, Shrewsbury, Barnes, Gunn (W.), Scotton, Flowers and Sherwin in England's eleven.

In yet one more respect do England and Australia maintain the fifty-fifty resemblance, for both sides have done the hat-trick three times. I hope to alter at least that symmetry before I retire!

While not professing to have any information as to the probable constitution of the Australian team of 1934, I anticipate that all of the following will make the tour, W. M. Woodfull (Capt.), V. Y. Richardson (Vice-Capt.), D. G. Bradman, S. J. McCabe, F. J. Fingleton, W. A. Oldfield, W. J. O'Reilly, T. Wall, L. Darling, L. P. O'Brien, L. H. Bromley, B. J. Tobin, P. K. Lee, possibly C. V. Grimmett, and a wicket-keeper, probably Walker.

Of these 15 men those who are not known to readers resident in England, the outstanding ones are the two left-handers, L. Darling and L. P. O'Brien; the medium slow right hand bowler, W. J. O'Reilly; another left-hander, H. Bromley; a useful all-rounder, P. K. Lee; B. J. Tobin a fastish right-hander, and J. Fingleton, who after making 23, 40, 83 and 1 in the first two Tests bagged a brace in the third and was dropped. Rather too readily so it seemed to me, seeing that in his very first innings against us, for New South Wales in November, he went right through the innings for 119 not out. The memory of that innings was wiped out by his doubleduck in the "atmosphere match" at Adelaide, and that was not, in my opinion, good judgment on the part of the selectors.

Fingleton is full of cricket, and I can see no reason why with his methods he should not make his full share of runs on our wickets. If it is decided not to bring Kippax, who I do not regard as being yet fit for the shelf, then Fingleton is the man for that vacancy. I shall be very greatly surprised if the Australian Board omit either O'Brien or Darling. The fact that both are left-handers is a very strong one in their favour.

Is there a bowler who really enjoys bowling to a left-hander? I wonder. I cannot say that I do, though, on the other hand, I do not particularly mind the "wrong way round" batsman. A left-handed batsman, granted that he is a good class one with a good head on his shoulders, must always have an unsettling effect on a right-handed bowler, particularly on one who is accustomed to get wickets caught on the slips or by the wicket keeper while the ball is new. So that a bowler has to keep a steady hold on himself whenever a left-hander gets set.

Because it has also to be remembered, that as on average a left-hander gets more bad length or badly directed balls than a right-hander he is more valuable to his side in the long run, than is a right handed bat of equal ability.

Here let me observe, in reply to the critics who say I bowl "at" my man, that in the fifth Test I bowled with four slips and a gully to the left-handers, none of whom were hit!! Of the three young left-handed Australians Bromley is at present the easiest to get out, because he is apt to "chance his arm" a bit. The other two, though both can force a bit, are steadier players. But I can foresee Bromley, once he gets set, making things very warm for the bowlers and interesting for the spectators.

Darling was beginning to be a nuisance in the Australian's second innings of the vital fourth Test when he was run out for 39 and he followed that with a very good 85 in the first innings of the next Test, so that he is certainly a dangerous customer.

I thought they dropped O'Brien too readily after his 10 and 11 in the second Test so that his 61 in the first innings, when he reappeared in the fifth Test, was not a surprise to me. Going in first with Woodfull for An Australian XI before the Test matches began O'Brien gave us reason to respect his ability as he made a good 46 before I bowled him. He is a brilliant field, and therefore sure to pull his weight on tour.

A definite weakness which may be beyond the Australian selectors to overcome rests in the fact that their chief bowlers are not batsmen.

Tobin is quite a fair batsman and I regard him as the most likely one and quite good enough with the ball to share the fast bowling with Wall.

Ironmonger is really past hope in either respect, though he would certainly reap his toll of wickets on our pitches, it would surprise him, more than anyone perhaps, if he totalled 50 runs on the whole tour. As a fielder I have never beheld Ironmonger's like, and I have heard many stories about the efforts in the field of Tom Wass, who was one of the greatest of Notts.' bowlers.

So I think we must rule out Ironmonger, now 46, and expect that the chief Australian bowlers will be O'Reilly, Wall or Tobin, perhaps both, Lee and possibly Grimmett, with McCabe and Bradman to help.

Ignoring the last two as bowlers, Lee, Tobin and Wall are the only ones of the others with any pretensions to bat. Between them in 18 Test match innings O'Reilly and Wall, made 124 runs all told. Therefore, short of a couple of discoveries during Australia's next season of 1933-34, or some wholly unexpected advancement in their batting, Australia will surely have the hutch door open at 7 wickets down in next season's Test matches. Failing the two eventualities I have named that is inevitable.

This means that a great responsibility will again rest on the first five or six who bat for Australia. Relatively a greater responsibility, because our own tail is not so incapable with the bat, than will be that which rests on the shoulders of our own first men. That is, at all events, how I view the probable state of affairs in the Test matches of next season.

In the past Australia has often found the man for the hour, but unless Grimmett, who is very keen to come on this tour, features a come-back this next season, Australia's tail should be Lee, Oldfield, Tobin; Wall, and O'Reilly. For patriotic reasons I hope my forecast materialises!

Dealing now with the real batting strength of Australia, viz.:– Woodfull, Richardson, Fingleton, Bradman, McCabe, Darling, O'Brien, and Bromley, it is, *without a Fast-Leg-Theory attack* against it, every bit as formidable as it was in 1930 in England. I have not the slightest doubt about this.

For one, Don Bradman is just as good a bat as he was then, and McCabe is really probably a better. Richardson will always be rather a doubtful quantity because of the slap-dash character of his methods. But all the same a very dangerous quantity, one whose retreating back all bowlers will be always glad to see.

Woodfull is not really one whit inferior now than he was in 1930, except that perhaps his defence is not quite the impregnable rock that England knows it to be. But a man who can play the 73 not out, carrying his bat through the second innings as he did in the "atmosphere match" at Adelaide, not to mention his 67 in the first innings of the fourth Test, and 67 in the second innings of the fifth Test, is still a first choice Test cricketer. His are not big scores if judged by the scoring in past rubbers and only when so judged. What we must do is to bear in mind always that this last was one of the lowest scoring rubbers in the history of the Ashes, since big totals came into vogue in 1892.

Before that year a 400 total was a very rare thing, a 500 almost unknown. Totals of from 150 to 300 were then the order of the Tests. 1892 produced 391, 307 and 499 in successive matches in Australia, to be followed by 334, 483, and 349 in successive matches in England. Then came 1894 with 586, 325, 437, 475, 333, 411, 284, 414, 385 and 298 in successive Tests, and by then good totals had become a habit.

On the last tour Australia, apart from 360 in the first innings of the first Test did not top 300 again until she made 340 in the first innings of the fourth and 435 in the first innings of the fifth. She had, on the other hand, successive totals of 164, 228, 191, 222, 193, and then the 340 followed by 175, 435 and 182.

From which it will be seen that Woodfull's chief scores were not those of failure in a season of big totals. If, as I expect he will be, Woodfull is here next summer, he should prove to be as tough a problem for the bowlers as he ever was.

McCabe was not always in the best of health, but nobody who can play such an innings as his 187 not out in the first Test · can be truly said to have lost batting ability.

There seemed to be a screw loose at times somewhere in McCabe's batting outfit, but where that is I am myself perhaps not sufficient of a batsman to say. I know that only once in his ten innings in these Tests did I get h.is wicket, and that was when Mr. Jardine caught him in the first innings at Adelaide. So perhaps my opinion on the point of whether McCabe has fallen off or not is a little prejudiced. At any rate I didn't notice the falling off!

Throughout this analysis I have omitted mention of Bill Ponsford. I should be very loth to say his career is ended. I feel that, if I was to write that, he is the most likely Australian to make a century in a Test. If so I would consume my words gladly. For at his best Ponsford was a very good bat indeed, and, except for that tendency to step too far across on the off-side and miss the straight ball on the leg stump a very sound one. He certainly overdid that stroke, which, though he got many runs from it, cost him his wicket on many occasions. I hesitate before suggesting they will not send him again but I believe that in view of the time having arrived for new blood, and especially for new blood with a bowling strain in it, Ponsford will not be a member of the next team.

Summing up the probable Australian XI of 1934, with the proviso-Leg-Theory barred, I assert that it will be every bit as difficult to beat on our wickets in four days as was that of 1930, or 1926.

If Leg-Theory is used then anything may happen.

Further than that I will not venture, except to assure my readers that, Fast-Leg-Theory or not, the rubber will not lack for keenness. In other words, book your seats now!

The dates of the Tests in 1934 are:–
Friday, June 8, 9, 11, 12 at Nottingham.
Friday, June 22, 23, 25, 26 at Lord's.
Friday, July 6, 7, 9, 10 at Manchester.

Friday, July 20, 21, 23, 24 at Leeds.

Saturday, August 18, 20, 21, 22 at Oval.

It will be seen that the third Test is at Manchester and not, as formerly, at Leeds.

The fifth Test will only be played to a finish if neither side has won two matches, or if the results after the fourth Test are equal. Those were the conditions contained in the Australian proposal, agreed to by the M.C.C.

WILL CRICKET COME TO THIS ?

CHAPTER XI

The Fast Bowler's Job

Physical fitness of stomach and consequently of wind and limb, which follow that fitness as night follows day, is absolutely the foundation of success in fast bowling.

It is just as well to have a good long run and a high overhead action, but, unless his stomach is in order, no fast bowler has the ghost of a chance of sustained success.

I write from acute personal experience and not from hearsay. I know quite well that I have been a different bowler after an operation in 1930 put right the internal trouble from which, unknown to me, I had been ailing.

I refer to that matter with some of my chief bowling figures in another chapter. Here I intend trying to help young bowlers along the right path, and also to assist my readers to look at the fast bowler's job from an angle from which perhaps they have never glanced at it. At all events not with a little more care than has the gentleman who wrote this year in a Sunday paper: "until Larwood took to bowling leg-side bumpers." That critic may take it from me that there is a very great deal more in Fast-Leg-Theory than the mere delivery of "leg-side bumpers" – a feat I should imagine of which any lusty yokel is capable.

I have discovered that even regular followers of the game do not always fully realise the extent of the physical strain which fast bowlers undergo.

For example, I measure out 12 good strides and when bowling top-speed actually deliver the ball off the fourteenth step.

My follow-up averages about five more steps. Thus the delivery of one ball takes from 19 to 20 running steps. Therefore, without any fielding to do, I have to walk back to the starting point, say another 25 yards from where I picked up the ball. So that, by the time I am ready to start my run for the *second* ball of an over I have already covered, say, 50 yards, since my running up strides are some of them more than three feet long.

Hence, on average, I run and walk 300 yards per over.

On the recent Australian tour I bowled exactly 210 overs in the five Tests. To do so I ran and walked 35.79 miles, or roughly 7 miles per match.

Spread over a whole match 7 miles is not so very much for a healthy man. But, taken by the day, and allowing for fielding between overs, the mental strain of bowling, and the additional physical strain, not reckoned in the total distance run and walked, required to deliver a ball at top speed, sometimes, as I had in Australia, with the skin off my toes, and towards the end of the tour with small bones fractured in one foot, and I think it will be readily agreed that fast bowling in Test cricket is no job for a weakling.

The foregoing figures should prove especially interesting if read at the same time as those of the fastest bowler of all time, Mr. C. J. Kortright, who wrote this year to a friend of mine the following interesting letter, which I have his permission to reproduce in full:

"I never really measured out my run up to the wicket, i.e. by stepping out a fixed number of paces from the wicket to the starting point, but, having fixed in my mind's eye *about* the required distance, I made a small mark and then arranged my run accordingly. On returning I would walk back to that mark and pivot round on the front part of my right boot, thus gradually working out a circular kickingoff hole somewhat resembling the shallow ragged mark that one might find on a putting green.

"As regards the distance of the run, I used to consider it about 18 yards. Frequently, on a fresh batsman coming in I would increase the distance by a yard or two for the first ball. This was mainly for two reasons, (i) to try to send down a yorker on the middle and leg stumps, to do which I found I required a little more space to straighten up and to thrust my left leg more forward, (ii) some men I knew coming in to take a first ball were inclined to be a little fidgety, and a slightly extended run added to the increased impetus, and besides was not warranted to soothe their nerves, more especially in the case of a novice making his debut.

"I always consider my run-up was much the same as that of poor old Tom Richardson, possibly a yard longer than his, as I noticed that we both started from more or less the same spot when Essex were playing Surrey. Bill Bradley, of Kent, was much about the same distance, though he of course started more from mid-off, running in diagonally. I mention these two because I played a good many times against both of them, and they were both rightly considered to be pretty 'swift.'"

The reader will find confirmation of Mr. Kortright's kindly endeavours for the benefit of incoming batsmen in Mr. J. W. Trumble's letter in another chapter. There the old Australian cricketer describes how Jarvis was, to use Mr. Kortright's phrase, "inclined to be a little fidgety," and the "pair" he bagged in the process.

From Mr. Kortright's letter we can get a line as to the physical stress entailed on such a big man as Tom Richardson in some of his matches, of which I give the following instances in the days of five-ball overs.

Year.	Place.	O.	M.	R.	W.	AV.	Result.
1893	Manchester	13·4	5	49	5	9·8	
	,,	44	15	107	5	21·4	Draw.

Year.	Place.	O.	M.	R.	W.	AV.	Result.
1894	Sydney	53·3	13	181	5	36·2	
	,,	11	3	27	1	27	Eng.
1895	Melbourne	23	6	57	5	11·4	
	,,	60	10	100	2	50	Eng.
	Adelaide	21	4	75	5	15	
	,,	31·2	8	89	3	29·6	Aust.
	Sydney	22	5	78	2	39	Aust.
	Melbourne	42	7	138	3	49·3	
	,,	45·2	7	104	6	17·3	Eng.
1896	Lord's	11·3	3	39	6	6·5	
	,,	47	15	134	5	26·8	Eng.
	Manchester	68	23	168	7	24	
	,,	42·3	16	76	6	12·6	Aust.
1896	Oval	5	0	22	0		
	,,	1	1	0	0		Eng.

Richardson went to Australia again in 1897-98 but, except in the fifth Test at Sydney when he bowled

O.	M.	R.	W.	AV.	Result.
36·1	7	94	8	11·7	
21·4	1	110	2	55	Aust.

he had passed his prime, and was not so successful.

Fancy bowling no overs in a Test match; as he did in 1896 at Manchester, and being on the losing side in spite of taking 13 wickets! That is regarded as the greatest fast bowling feat of all Test cricket. A wonderful performance on the part of a giant over six feet and over sixteen stones in weight. I, for one, take off my cap to my great predecessor, whose figures I quote so fully here as proof for my young readers of what can be done by a fast bowler, because it has been done and so can be done again.

With an 18 yards "run" Richardson, with his follow-up, must have run and walked about 65 yards per ball, or 325 yards per five-ball over. Or, just over 20 miles running and walking in that memorable three-day match at Manchester, in which the hours were 11.30 to 6.30 on the second and third days, and 12 to 6.30 on the first. Not, as now, 11.30 to 6.30 first day and 11.0 to 6.30 for the next three.

These figures and happenings showing the physical stress incurred by a fast bowler in Test cricket, may serve to give the cricket-lover an inkling as to why all suggestions for longer hours of play and for the abolition of the tea-interval receive scant favour from those who are playing cricket six days a week nonstop for four and a half months. Doubtless it is very annoying for the office-worker to arrive at a ground just in time to see the players reaching the pavilion for their sometimes sorely needed quarter of an hour for the tea-interval, but the county game is for the player first, last, and all the time, and not for the officeworker.

It is true that not all the eleven in the field have walked and run five or six miles by tea time, apart from other fielding exercise and mental strain, but the regulations as to hours of play must, and do, cope first with the needs of those players upon whom the game is the severest physical strain. That is to say, the fast bowlers and the wicket keepers. The fast bowlers are an easy first in this particular competition, especially those who are under either a thoughtless or a ruthless captain.

In this respect at all events my life has been indeed a happy one – I cannot of course speak for any fast bowler among any of the great ones of a bygone time. But, if any one of them, either for their county or for England, ever had more kind consideration than that which I have enjoyed under Messrs. A. W. Carr, D. R. Jardine and A. P. F. Chapman, then indeed can he account himself lucky. I cannot remember ever having been overbowled, or asked to continue when either I was tiring or was out of luck.

I know that I owe a great deal of my success to my captains and most gratefully do I here acknowledge that fact. I trust that my successors in the Notts. and England elevens, when it is my turn to be an onlooker, are equally lucky.

Throughout my career I have never asked to be taken off, but if ever I have felt that it was in the interests of the side that I should not continue, and have spoken to my captain to that effect, I have never spoken in vain.

Quite apart from the mere physical effort of putting all in one's bowling a fast bowler must also sustain wear on the mental side of the process of bowling. I am afraid some people assume a little too readily that only slow and slow-medium bowlers scheme and think! I gather this from such remarks as that I quote at the beginning of this chapter, since the bowling of "leg-side bumpers" requires, I should guess, a minimum of intelligence. If only slow bowlers think what they are doing what a brainless lot of people we fast bowlers must be!

Elsewhere in this book I write of my duels with Bradman. Here let me assure my readers that when bowling to him my share of the battle was certainly not one of brute force and something ignorance. The bowler who is confronted by Bradman and doesn't think doesn't bowl for long. Mere

3 Photographs of Bradman, trying all sorts of shots to combat the leg side attack, the bottom picture is the only time that Bradman was hit.

getting rid of the ball, leg-side bumpers for example, cuts very little ice when in opposition to such a cool and practised player as Don. That fellow is a very long way from being the "cocktail cricketer" which Warwick Armstrong in a rather uncouth sneer styled him last season. Apart from his wonderful eye and wrists Don has a very quick thinking brain. To him leg-side bumpers would be mere gift fours as often as any bowler was fool enough, and incompetent enough, to serve them up.

Don has not finished with me yet! I believe I am supposed to have mastered him. I wish I was as sure of the mastery as, apparently, are those who have presented me with it. I hope the duel will be resumed next season, and that everybody will come to watch it. I promise here and now to do all in my power to make it interesting.

I wrote just now that it is a popular view that only slow and medium-slow bowlers scheme and think! I give the lie direct on behalf of my fellow fast-bowlers and myself to any such groundless theory. I have always given as much thought to how to get out my different opponents as I possibly could, ever since I had the good fortune to enter the ranks of first-class cricket permanently. Never do I bowl the same to two different batsmen, except when I cross my field over from the slips to the leg-side. On the leg-side one's bowling has more of similarity – therefore I am afraid of monotony for the onlooker, not for the batsman! – than it has when a slips field is set.

For one thing, and I may write this without giving away state secrets of my stock-in-trade, I attempt to bowl more yorkers when I have a slip field than when Leg-Theory is in operation.

My theory is that when I have several slips the class batsman is always chary of the swerving-away ball, which is, of necessity, pitched either a good length, or just short of a good length. Consequently, he gets into a habit of "leaving alone." That being so he is at the same time very keenly on the look-out for anything like an over-pitched ball. All the more so because when I have four slips and a deep third-man there is often a gap somewhere between gully and mid-off. A good batsman waits, *because he knows how to wait,* for the slightly over-pitched ball which is, to him, an assured four through that gap.

Now, that is precisely the frame of mind which ripens him for making the error, which we bowlers want him to make, of mistaking a yorker for a half-volley.

By this process of reasoning I base the theory that a slips setting of the field is more favourable for the bowling of a yorker than is a leg-side setting of the field. There the bowler seldom gets the batsman into the desired frame of mind favourable to the bowling of a yorker.

Because, that being the blind-side of the batsman, very few batsmen have the straight drive past mid-on in their armoury and for that reason alone, would block rather than try to hit an attempted yorker. They would thus try to do the very thing which no bowler wants them to do with a yorker.

A yorker, let me impress upon, at all events, my younger readers, depends for its success upon being mistaken for a half-volley and, therefore, of being hit at.

Thus, it is seen that the yorker bowled when it is a leg-side field is a waste of energy if the batsman is worthy the name. And of all the players on the field the fast bowler is the one who, least of all, can afford to waste energy.

This is not to say that my counsel is, *never* bowl the yorker when there is a leg-side disposition of the field. As a variant it is a good thing. As a means of unsettling a batsman who is, perhaps, already a bit rattled by being, as it were, the centre of a squad of policemen, it is a good thing. Just as anything, done fairly, to rattle any batsman is a good thing.

But on the whole, owing to the odds being heavily against its success, for reasons given I do not advise the yorker as a weapon in the battery of the Fast-Leg-Theory bowler.

Writing generally of the art of fast bowling the first thing I advise an ambitious youngster to acquire is Accuracy. By accuracy I mean both of Length *and Direction.* What is the use of bowling a good Length if it is so wide of the wicket that a *good* batsman will ignore it? Wickets don't fall from the skies.

Direction is really Width. A really fast bowler who habitually pitches a good Length *and* Width must succeed. Success is for him inevitable. Width means that nearness to the line of the off and the leg stumps which *compels* a stroke.

As a general rule for guidance it is a bad ball in all respects when a batsman is able to leave it alone *of his own accord.* A ball played at and missed comes under quite a different category. So that young bowlers must drill themselves into bowling as few balls as possible that the batsman *intentionally* does not play. Let the young bowler be his own critic, and say to himself: "He is seeing it all the way, and is purposely ignoring it, therefore *I am bowling badly.*" In other words, make the batsman play at the ball. Even if a four results from his playing remember that he might have offered a catch. Whereas, if he purposely ignores the ball you, the bowler, have walked and run about fifty yards and used up some mental energy into the bargain, all for nothing.

Now, with regard to a fast bowler's action and run. It is extraordinary that opinions differ slightly with regard to the length of the latter but most agree about the former. I dismiss the matter of the Action by saying that the higher, i.e. the more overhead, the better, so long as the bowler does not "lie down" in order to bring his arm over straight.

As to the Run, *most emphatically a long one is absolutely essential.*

From the beginning of first-class cricket the very best fast bowlers have all had long runs, delivering the ball from anything between the 13th and the 17th or 18th step. I need only mention Tom Richardson, Bill Lockwood, Arnold Warren, and Messrs. C. J. Kortright and N. A. Knox, each of whom I never saw, but have often heard and read about, of a bygone generation, and George Hirst, E. A. Macdonald and J. M. Gregory since the War. Not one of these bowled off less than his 11th step. Of these only Gregory, and I believe Mr. Knox, had a laboured or awkward action.

All the others had a flowing fast or fastish run, with a high overhead delivery. And all of them were masters of their art, to emulate any of whom should be the aim of every youngster.

I am not to be drawn into a discussion on the subject of who was the fastest of them all, but if the stories from authentic sources about the pace of Mr. Kortright are not legends then the rest of us must certainly play second fiddle. At all events I have never knocked a stump out of the ground and sent it twirling over the wicket-keeper's head, he standing twelve yards back, as Mr. Kortright did at Lord's – a feat for verification of which there is ample obtainable evidence in the persons of the bowler himself, and of Mr. Percy Perrin, who was playing in the match.

I counsel all aspiring young fast bowlers to cultivate an easy high delivery with a long steady run with no jumping and springing about, because all of that is waste of energy which hinders rather than helps accuracy. Then, let the final swing be with the body as sideways as possible in order to get leverage from the loins.

Do not *always* deliver from the same distance from the bowler's wicket. Let your run end sometimes near the leg-stump, sometimes near the return-crease, and now and then a foot short of the bowling-crease. Each of these things is apt to upset the batsman and thus to bring about a mistimed stroke.

In practice mark a place about a foot square on the wicket at about seven yards from the wicket at which you are bowling. Until you can keep on hitting that you have not got the necessary accuracy. As soon as you have acquired the habit of pitching the ball on or close to that square foot you will find that you may then – and not until then – begin to practise, with some hope of success, the finer arts of break and swerve. Both of these are secondary matters. Indeed, swerve comes a long way last of the three.

Swerve is useless until you have acquired such control of the ball as will enable you to pitch it on or near that square, or on or quite close to the batting crease when you want bowl a yorker.

Most young bowlers put the cart before the horse and practise sending down swerves before they have learned to bowl the ball *where they want to bowl it!* That is bad alike for them and for the future bowling strength of County cricket, not to mention England cricket.

No coach is justified in showing a youngster the grip for swerve bowling until that youngster has mastered the art of pitching a plain straight ball on or near the square patch painted on the pitch. It is the coaches who do not insist on Length and Direction first who do bowling harm. Since, through those two qualities we get Accuracy. Without which Bowling is not Bowling.

CHAPTER XII

My Home at Trent Bridge.

INTRODUCED BY JOE HARDSTAFF – A FEW WRINKLES FOR YOUNG PROFESSIONALS – A GREAT TRIO, MR. ARTHUR CARR, JIMMY IREMONGER AND GEORGE GUNN – MY SEVEN SEASONS' BAG OF WICKETS – SOME STAR BATSMEN – THE LAST OVER.

Some of my readers may think that in writing at the end of this book about my early days in big cricket I have put the cart before the horse.

I am well aware that the main interests in this work are not Larwood's apprenticeship in first-class cricket, but Fast-Leg-Theory and the recent Australian tour. I expect and hope, however, that the verdict will be that I haven't written out the batting order of my chapters so badly after all.

I began, like most youngsters on a county ground, in fear and trembling and not very comfortable boots.

I was not long in getting over the first, as everybody at Trent Bridge was so good to me, but it would seem from my experiences at Melbourne in the second Test that I have not even now quite got over the second!

By the way, as a sidelight on what players on tour sometimes have to go through I must mention that after the Melbourne boots incident I was never really comfortable about the feet until a parcel from Nottingham containing the right kind of boots arrived just in time for the fifth Test. That was due to a little bit of foresight on the part of folks at home, for which I was very thankful. They *do* think of us sometimes when we are far away from our own hearths, and receiving the compliments of the season from strangers!

I was recommended to the county club by Joe Hardstaff, to whom I can never be grateful enough. Joe was always most encouraging, and has always been a good friend. He is one of the world's very best umpires to-day. I wonder sometimes, when I think of straight men like our Joe, whether it is really a good rule that no umpire shall stand in a match in which his late county is taking part. I have bowled sometimes in Test matches from his end and I have never the least doubt that if I had to appeal for a catch or a leg-before-wicket I would just as soon rely upon Joe's decision as upon that of any umpire anywhere, whether it was for or against me. I wish I might give here his opinion on the "Thought-Reader," but I don't want to scorch these pages, much less to reduce them to Ashes!

At Trent Bridge everyone soon made me feel at home though, of course, a stranger has to prove himself. At that time Fred Barrett was going very strong, and there was also Matthews who was a pretty good one at a fast pace.

I did not sign on with any stupid ideas n my head about walking into the county eleven, so I was not in the least worried when, after a year or so, I was still without any hint of being invited to make my first appearance.

Here I would like to say a word to all young professionals who may be similarly situated and who find themselves fidgeting about on the fringe of their county eleven. They will be much happier if they realise three things once and for all.

First, that they are engaged in a game of Patience which may never work out as expected. Secondly, that Class will *always* come to the top – no county club *ever by any chance fails* to include in its eleven a Class cricketer if he is a professional.

Thirdly, and especially in the case of wicketkeepers and fast-bowlers, who are naturally in a big minority in an eleven, there is always the matter of Luck.

The worst attitude a young professional can assume is one of grousing and grumbling because he is not chosen for his county's eleven.

That frame of mind never ends by placing its owner's head inside an England cap.

To use an expression used elsewhere in this book young cricketers must take the rough with the smooth. Grumbling and sulking never got a cricketer into his county's XI, and I am not able to state whether any professional ever played for England without having first proved himself in his county team. Probably the one player who played least in county cricket before playing for England was Sid Barnes, but I may be wrong about this.

County clubs do not keep players on their ground staffs for the sake of their looks. The club is always ready enough to include a good cricketer in its eleven but it is only the player himself who, by his deeds out on the middle and not by his excuses in the dressing-room, can *compel* the club to play him. Therefore, until those deeds are performed, since they are the only things which concern the county-club selectors, the cricketer cannot reasonably expect the invitation to play for his county. That is the game of Patience.

Both the player and his county selectors are only waiting for the deeds. The player believes he is good enough, and that belief is shared by the selectors or the player would not be in the pay of the club. All that is needed is the delivery of the goods, that is to say the wickets, the runs, the catches, and the run-outs. Dealing with my second point – Class. I need only quote the cases of Hobbs, Woolley, Hendren, Sutcliffe, Hearne and George Gunn. I believe it is a fact that after their very first appearance for their county they have never been left out of the eleven except for injury or ill-health. There may be other similar cases, but these suffice to prove my statement that Class will *always* tell.

In other words any young players who are upset at not being regular members of their county elevens may take it from me that, however good players they may be, there is one thing they lack and that is, beyond all doubt, the touch of Class which decides the matter in spite of themselves, or anything that they may say or do.

Now, writing of the special cases of wicketkeepers and fast bowlers. I can best illustrate this by asking any restless young wicket-keeper what would happen supposing that to-day Ames, Duckworth and Lilley were all on the Trent Bridge staff? Only the accident of birth prevents such a possibility from being a fact.

That I am not imagining too much is shown from the experience of the Surrey club a few years before the war. For wicket-keeper they had available at the same time Strudwick (England), Sullivan (later Glamorgan}, W. B. Franklin (Cambridge University and Gentlemen) and Livesey, who afterwards qualified for Hants. The man in possession, Strudwick, was too good and physically too sound to be movable. I have been told that the Surrey club were freely blamed for "letting Sullivan and Livesey go." Actually, the Surrey club performed a kind act in their cases. By acting as they did both these men played a lot of county cricket with success.

There may be other instances as, for example, at Old Trafford where such a capable wicket-keeper-batsman as Farrimond is on the Lancashire staff with Duckworth. I never hear of the case of a good class professional wicketkeeper who cannot get his county cap because the man with the gloves retains his form without my deep sympathy going out for the one who must be called the second string, though perhaps, if put to the proof, he might show himself the better man of the two.

Hard cases there must always be on most ground staffs, but if anything I write has any influence I advise all such to be plucky and stick it out. Luck is not always one-sided.

From the very outset of my career at the headquarters of a great county club I have had the greatest· encouragement, my acquaintance with my captain, Mr. Carr, with Jimmy Iremonger and with George Gunn developing, may I say it, into terms of close friendship.

Most gratefully do I acknowledge the value of their advice from the very beginning right up to the present day.

Nobody but myself knows how much I owe to Mr. Carr for the very careful way in which, when my health was not of the best up to the end of the season of 1930 and since, he has always considered nursing my strength. It is a very big thing for a fast-bowler to feel quite sure that his captain will never "bowl him to death," and that even if it is a losing match he will not be kept on an over too long. Also, it is a most heartening feeling to have that if one feels a bit off-colour one could go to the captain and say so without being suspected of shirking one's job. From the first day I bowled under his orders Mr. Carr has been most thoughtful on my behalf. I have never made a suggestion to him on the field to have it turned down without a thought.

Though the following case concerns me only partly I must mention it here because it directly concerns fast bowling. There seems to be a notion that fast bowlers are only "out to hurt," and that the main idea of some captains is to encourage them in this playful little habit. In a match in Essex a year or two ago, the pitch was thought to be so inadequate that Mr. Carr suggested to the Essex captain that neither of them should use their fast bowlers. This was acceded to, and in that game the fast bowlers earned their money easily! It helped a little to atone for some of those games in which I have run several miles while bowling, without getting a wicket. My Skipper, Mr. Arthur Carr, has been kind enough to write me the following appreciation for my "Home" Chapter. He writes:–

"I shall always remember 'Loll' (that's what we all call him) bowling at the nets for the first time. I asked who he was and was told his name is Larwood. Little did I think then that he was to become the present day finest fast bowler in the world. He was a tiny little fellow, very polite, serious, most retiring, but with both eyes and ears wide open. I never thought he would become what he is as he was so small, and although he put the devil into his bowling, I was afraid he would never last in County Cricket.

"When he did come into the side I used to bowl him four or five overs, but now I have known him bowl for an hour and a half on end. In fact last year he bowled through the two innings to Leicester without a rest, an amazing performance.

"When 'Loll' first played for Notts. whenever he hit the stumps a broad smile came across his face which he tried to conceal. It did not interest him if somebody was caught off his bowling!

"When the Selection Committee picked him to play for England under self in 1926 – I told him. He replied quietly: – 'Surely Skipper, I am not good enough to play for England.' He has always been so modest.

" 'Loll' has a most determined character, he is full of grit, and the moment he steps on the field he is a trier till the Close of Play. When we drop his catches we all want to sink into the ground, but we know that it is only his keenness that makes him a 'little short with us'!

"Any catch in the slips off Larwood is a fine catch; the public do not realise this by their groans when they are dropped.

"*Knowing Larwood as I do* the finest thing for England that Australia ever did was to 'barrack' him in these last Tests as this would make him bowl better than ever, which he did. If anything upsets him he bowls twice as well. As I have said before, there is no more determined character and no man could have a better friend than 'Loll.' I hope his book is a very best seller."

As for Jimmy Iremonger I can hardly say too much. He has been like a father to me at Trent Bridge. Certainly he has taught me any batting I know. I hope it will interest him to know that during my innings of 98 in the fifth Test at Sydney I thought of him, as I felt that not a few of the runs were his.

If anyone has got a spark of cricket in him old Jimmy will fan it into something like a fire and then, of course, it rests with the youngster. Jimmy's style of bowling, medium-slow righthand, with a perfect length, a bit of off-break, varied with a little go-with-the-arm, is, to my mind, the very ideal for a coach. A coach should not bowl fast to teach a colt strokes, and to encourage him to make them the sound way. The first thing a coach should have is Length. Jimmy has got a cast-iron pattern of that. If what the cricket world refers to as the old-fashioned Notts. bowlers bowled a more consistent length than Jimmy then they weren't men, they were machines. I know nobody in first-class cricket to-day who can bowl the ball he wants to bowl with the regularity with which Jimmy can do this. Being able to do that enables him really to coach a young cricketer, as it is not much use trying to teach a boy a stroke and then to bowl a ball off which it is impossible to make the stroke which is being taught. It will be a very sad day for Notts. cricket, and for all of *us*, when Jimmy's time for retiring arrives. It is not necessary for me to write much about such public property as the cricket of George Gunn, who surely will be always remembered as one of the most accomplished and masterly batsmen of all time.

I, for one Notts. bowler, am only thankful he was a Notts. batsman! For I know only too well that if he had been a few years younger and the No. 1 of another county he would not have been long in showing me what's wrong with Fast-Leg-Theory.

I never saw the bowler who really bothered George. He had a stroke for every ball in the game. Few batsmen in my experience have got more fours with less effort than he. Even if he did not score his never-failing easy-going temperament never did anything to upset his side and make them think that there were hidden terrors in either the wicket or the bowling. While, when he succeeded, which was not seldom, he really made the bowling so easy that even the greatest coward. among us got that "fifty feeling" before he had begun to buckle on his pads.

I never heard George say a word in the way of belittling an opponent. I have been told that even in 1921, when Notts. supporters were so sore at him not being chosen for the Test match on our own ground, there was never a grumble from him. Although then he was simply full of runs, and years after that was making hundreds off the very best bowling in this country.

There is a story that when Gunn was in Australia playing in a Test Cotter bowled his fastest short one, which George flicked to the square-leg boundary. Cotter tried it again, same result. George was then more or less of an unknown, at all events in Australia. Crossing between overs Cotter remarked: "If you do that again, you young beggar, I'll bowl your block off!"

"Just as you like," said George quietly.

Cotter did it again, and the ball went same road. In the end George had his hundred all right.

Some years after the war George spent a memorable birthday, part of it on the Southampton ground. He had got about 70 without a mistake and had made all the bowlers wish they were out yachting or something.

"Here Alec, give me that ball," said Lord Tennyson cheerily, to Kennedy, "*I'll* put a stop to this!" and the Hampshire captain proceeded to bowl the fastest theory he could. George took 18 off the first over to all parts of the field, and I forget how many off the second, whereupon his lordship wisely retired to deep mid-off and let Alec try again. George got 180 odd that day.

I look upon George Gunn as quite one of the world's greatest batsmen, ranking him certainly as the equal, in his own way, with Hobbs or Woolley, or Macartney, or Bradman. I should be surprised if anyone in Nottinghamshire disagreed with me on this point and I know that many out of my county are of my opinion. I owe a debt of gratitude to "Tangy"

Harold Larwood with his wife Lois, and baby June, the first of his five daughters.

Voce who has always been a good pal to me, on and off the field. Out on the middle it is always: "How's the wind? Here, this end'll suit you best, Harold," when Mr. Carr has left the choice to us. A magnificent field, "Tangy" may some day settle down into something of a forcing bat. He is not a lucky bowler for he bowls more balls with which the batsman can do nothing, without getting his wicket, than almost anyone I know. Payton, who has now retired, was for years the best No. 5 in England, just as Lilley has been for years one of the best-class wicketkeepers and never an easy wicket to get. I hope very much that Willis Walker has the three finest days of this season for his well-earned benefit. Always a sound player he has many and many a time "made" the innings when George has got out early.

"Buster" Keeton, about the fastest runner between wickets in England, is training on into a very useful No. 2. With his pace he is always a fine field. In "young George," Harris and Hardstaff, Notts. has three young players than whom I doubt if any county can name three young ones who collectively are as good.

And the two Staples must complete my tale, a brace of real utility cricketers who are, either or both of them, always up to something getting useful runs or wickets almost all the time. Take us all round we're a very happy family at Trent Bridge. A bit of a trial at times, no doubt, to Shaw, who fathers us so well. I don't really know what we should do without him, but this I am sure of: if he had been at Melbourne I'd never have had that bother with my boots. The fact is, he spoils us so, most of us don't know how to look after our own cricket gear. The only thing we do watch is that nobody takes our pet bat by mistake. Yes, even the tail-enders watch their bats as keenly as do any of the people who make two or three thousand runs a season as a habit. That's a curious, but quite true, fact about a cricket team, though I never heard that Tom Wass ever took a bat with him to a match. Perhaps, being such an optimist by nature, he did. If so, any one who borrowed it would know.

To turn now to my early days out on the middle of the ground which is the most important bit of the world to a cricketer.

I went through all the usual life of a youngster on a county cricket ground, never wanting for advice! This was showered on me, sometimes by folks who I don't think ever played cricket, and, of course, by a good many who had. I am afraid a good deal of both was in at one ear and out at the other.

I was much more concerned about the nails in my boots and my bat getting the right amount of drinks of linseed oil to trouble my head about talk.

I played in lots of club and ground matches and got a few wickets, and I did not have to wait long for my chance.

After playing only once for Notts. In 1924 I actually got my head inside an England cap in 1926.

I shall always believe that the late Johnny Tyldesley helped me. He was playing for Lancashire's Second Eleven – he was coach at Old Trafford after his retirement – in a game at Kirkby in 1925, which was a very memorable one for me. Notts. second were playing Lancashire second and I took 8 for 44. In that Lancashire second eleven were Iddon and Sibbles of the present eleven. I was then 18, and soon afterwards, getting into the county eleven in the middle of June, I think I may say that I soon became a regular member of it. I took 73 wickets for Notts. that season.

Here are my figures in the general averages, and for Notts., since and including 1925. The first line gives my Notts., and the second my general average.

	Place	O.	M.	R.	W.	AV.
1926	1	693·1	164	1,755	96	18·28
	6	974·1	217	2,509	137	18·31

	Place	O.	M.	R.	W.	AV.
1927	1	543·2	126	1,500	91	16·48
	1	629	147	1,695	100	16·95
1928	1	669	163	1,636	116	14·10
	1	834·5	204	2,003	138	14·51
1929*	2	496·3	101	1,475	80	18·43
	25	871·1	182	2,535	117	21·66
1930	1	444	90	1,125	89	12·64
	4	621	124	1,622	99	16·38
1931	1	535·3	111	1,294	105	12·32
	1	651·3	142	1,553	129	12·03
1932	1	684·4	162	1,639	141	11·62
	1	866·4	203	2,084	162	12·86

*Notts. won the championship this year, and " Tangy " Voce was first in the bowling averages with 107 wickets for 16·03 apiece.

This gives the following result for my first seven seasons as a regular member of the Notts. XI.

	Wickets.	Runs.	Average.
Notts.	718	10,424	14·5
All	882	14,001	15·8

Or a yearly average of

	Wickets.	Runs.	Average.
Notts.	102	1,488	14.5
All	140	2,000	14.2

Here I might mention that I have been hit for six only three times in my career. In 1928, Vic Richardson did so for South Australia v. M.C.C. In 1929, Ames did so for Kent at Trent Bridge. In 1933, H. Gamble did so for Queensland v. M.C.C. at Brisbane.

In my seven seasons I have thus headed our county averages six times, and those of the whole country's averages four times.

In regard to the whole averages I must say that I have not included in those any, what I call, "casual" bowlers, or anyone who bowled less than 250 overs during the whole season. I hope this will be considered fair.

In Test cricket I first made a mark at the Oval, when we won the Ashes in 1926. Mr. Chapman had been suddenly brought in to captain the team and he captained splendidly, acting on his own though never hesitating, if he wanted it, to ask advice from Wilfrid Rhodes or Jack Hobbs.

I should like to mention here how very glad I am I can say that I played for England on the same side as Rhodes.

He must have been indeed a magnificent bowler at his best. I know that in that game he had the Australians guessing "all roads," as we say in Nottingham. They took the wrong turning so often that he took 2 for 35 and 4 for 44, at the age of 43, and between us we were able to deliver the goods.

At that time I was well under eleven stones weight, and, as I have never stood 5 feet 8 inches high, some may no doubt wonder where I get my pace from! Well, a youngster has to use his arms and his loins and his back muscles in the mine where I used to work, and, as in proportion to the rest of me my arms are long, and I have always been active in movement, to bowl at a fast pace is only second nature to me.

In that year I played in my first Test. It was at Lord's on an even paced, felt-like, wicket, and I took 2 for 99 and 1 for 37 and did not bat. The match was drawn, Australia making 383, Bardsley going right through the innings for 193, and 194 for five; England 475 for four declared, Hobbs 119 and Hendren 127 not out.

I was not chosen for the next Test, at Leeds, when Macartney made a hundred before lunch, and Macaulay's and Geary's batting saved England from a crushing defeat. Nor was I "revived" for the fourth Test at Old Trafford. But I played at the Oval and took 3 for 82 and 3 for 34.

The Australians were very badly captained in our second innings while the ball was turning.

A. J. Richardson, who should not be confused with Victor Richardson of the present time, was allowed to bowl long spells round the wicket, with several fielders in the shortleg area, to Hobbs and Sutcliffe. That, of course, did us good, as our two best batsmen simply tided over the time when the wicket was helping the bowlers, and both eventually got a century. Another tactical mistake was in allowing their only left-hander, Macartney, on a pitch made for a left-hander, to bowl over the wicket. The result was that whenever his spin, pitching on the wicket, beat the bat it missed the wicket. He beat the bat several times without getting a wicket. His actual bowling was very good, but his bowling over the wicket in that innings was one of the most outstanding instances in my experience of a left-hander throwing away a gift such as is rare.

If Macartney had bowled round the wicket in that innings, and Richardson over the wicket, Australia would most likely have won that game.

Although it was seven years ago I remember that Test very clearly. There had been rain about mid-day on the last day, followed by a very hot August sun. The Australians made a mistake putting the heavy roller on. Such decisions have to be made very quickly. The idea was to bring up from the turf as much wet as possible in order to make our fast bowling slower, and to prevent our slow bowlers from breaking the ball. But the heavy roller brought up just enough moisture to make the top of the wicket a bit "cakey," with firm soil underneath. I was able to make the ball rise sharply, and at the same time Rhodes could make it turn quickly.

I got Woodfull at once well caught by George Geary at "gully," and Macartney was also caught by George for 16. Rhodes then worried Ponsford and Collins out, and to all intents and purposes we had won the Ashes. Tate made a fine one-hander at short-leg off a shorter ball from me, and, Rhodes getting Bardsley caught at slip, the innings was over.

Except for the year 1930 I have generally done fairly well in Test cricket, though better since my health improved after 1930. On the Australian tour of 1928-29 I was not at my best except at Brisbane, partly on account of my health, and partly because, being young, I suppose I bothered more about the treatment dealt out to me by the rowdy and ill-mannered elements round the ground, than I did on the last tour. I felt sometimes during the last tour that I could never have stood such treatment had I had it four and five years ago.

In the course of my seven years' active cricket, I have rubbed shoulders with, or in other ways challenged the batting ability of, some pretty good players.

It may surprise some of my readers if I state my opinion that out of the whole crowd of them, I find Sandham of Surrey the most difficult batsman to get out.

It will be seen that I am not writing without the book when I quote Sandham's figures against Notts., out and home, from 1926 to 1932, inclusive. 19 innings, 1,238 runs, 65.1 average, highest score 152. In that period he has made four centuries and three scores of 92 and two over 50. In those 19 innings I have bowled him only twice and had him caught off me three times, so that "Andy" has given me plenty to think about. I regard him as a world's batsman. He is one of the best cutters in the game, and is always as sound as a bell.

Among Englishmen I choose him, Woolley, George Gunn, Hobbs, Sutcliffe, Ernest Tyldesley and Hendren as the pick, with Sutcliffe as, next to Sandham, the most difficult to get out. The best Australian batsmen in my career have been Macartney, easily first, Bradman, Bardsley, the late Archie Jackson, Vic Richardson, Ponsford, McCabe, and Woodfull in 1926.

My favourite ground is Trent Bridge, and next to that Lord's and Hove.

And so I arrive at the last over.

The umpires have had a glance at the clock. Soon the streets will be echoing with: "Close of Play."

It is indeed a comforting thought that there can never be a final "Close" of play.

This great game will go on for ever, in spite of everything, in spite of its few enemies within and without, in spite of each and every passing cloud. Before I was born it was rent with dissensions about Throwing and about the length of the over.

Then followed keen discussions and serious proposed legislation about the L.B.W. Law. The size of the wicket, the weight and the size of the ball, and, more recently, the Declaration Law with all kinds of fantastic and impossible, not to say stupid, proposals for brightening the game, have followed each other.

Until, as though tired out at legislating concerning things seen, it is now proposed to pass a law which to work at all can only work if one man can guess right as to what is going on in the mind of another during a split second of time. It looks as though someone only framed that proposal to make things more difficult!

At any rate, I can complete this last over by wishing Cricket a happy issue out of such tomfoolery with complete confidence.

Appendix

As a curiosity at the end of the book I give the cables sent by the Australian Board of Control to the M.C.C. who were thus forced to reply to communications which should never have been written, much less sent.

THE AUSTRALIAN BOARD OF CONTROL'S CABLE. JAN. 18th, 1933.

"Body-Line bowling has assumed such proportions as to menace the best interests of the game, making protection of the body by the batsmen the main consideration. This is causing intensely bitter feeling between the players, as well as injury. In our opinion it is unsportsmanlike. Unless stopped at once, it is likely to upset the friendly relations existing between Australia and England."

To the remark that Body-Line bowling "is causing intensely bitter feeling between the players" I can myself give an unqualified denial.

Further, as reported from Canberra on May 3rd, Bill Oldfield said there in the course of a public address: "There was always a spirit of cordiality between the two teams."

Thus, out of the mouth of their own wicket-keeper, and as straight a player as ever breathed, the Board of Control's first cable stands condemned for what it really is-utter humbug.

MARYLEBONE CRICKET CLUB'S REPLY. JAN. 23rd, 1933.

"We, Marylebone Cricket Club, deplore your cable.

"We deprecate your opinion that there has been unsportsmanlike play.

"We have fullest confidence in captain, team and managers, and are convinced that they would do nothing to infringe either the laws of cricket, or the spirit of the game.

"We have no evidence that our confidence has been misplaced. Much as we regret accidents to Woodfull and Oldfield, we understand that in neither case was the bowler to blame.

"If the Australian Board of Control wish to propose a new law or rule, it shall receive our careful consideration in due course. We hope the situation is not now as serious as your cable would seem to indicate, but if it is such as to jeopardise the good relations between English and Australian cricketers, and you consider it desirable to cancel remainder of programme, we would consent, but with great reluctance."

(Signed),

FINDLAY, Secretary.

THE A. B. C.'s SECOND CABLE. JAN. 30th, 1933.

"We appreciate your difficulty in dealing with this matter without having seen the actual play. We unanimously regard 'body-line' bowling, as adopted in some games in the present tour, as opposed to the spirit of cricket, and unnecessarily dangerous to the players. We are deeply concerned that the ideals of the game shall be preserved, and we have therefore appointed a committee to report on the means necessary to eliminate such bowling from Australian cricket, beginning with the 1933-34 season. We will forward its recommendations for your consideration and hope for your co-operation in their application to all cricket. We do not consider it necessary to cancel the remainder of the programme."

It was stated at the same time that this was despatched that, subject to them agreeing to serve, Messrs. R. J. Hartigan (Queensland) Chairman; M. A. Noble (N.S.W.), W. M. Woodfull (Victoria), and V. Y. Richardson (South Australia) should compose the special committee.

THE SECOND REPLY. FEB. 2nd, 1933.

"We, the committee of the Marylebone Cricket Club, note with pleasure that you do not consider it necessary to cancel the remainder of programme, and that you are postponing the whole issue until after the present tour is completed.

"May we accept this as a clear indication that the good sportsmanship of our team is not in question?

"We are sure you will appreciate how impossible it would be to play any Test match in the spirit we all desire unless both sides were satisfied there was no reflection upon their sportsmanship. When your recommendation reaches us it shall receive our most careful consideration and will be submitted to the Imperial Cricket Conference."

(Signed), FINDLAY,
Secretary.

THE A. B. C.· FINAL CABLE. FEB. 8th, 1933.

"WE DO NOT REGARD THE SPORTSMAN SHIP OF YOUR TEAM AS BEING IN QUESTION.

"Our position was fully considered at the recent Sydney meeting, and is as indicated in our cable of January 30th.· It is the particular class of bowling referred to therein which we consider not in the best interests of cricket, and in this view we understand we are supported by many eminent English cricketers. We join heartily with you in hoping the remaining Tests will be played with the traditional good feelings."

Nearly three months later, having lost the Ashes, the A.B.C.'s Special Committee frame a special Law of Cricket, which the A.B.C. pass for use in Australia, the said Law being aimed solely to prevent such utterly unsportsmanlike tactics as fast bowling bowled "with intent to injure." If the A.B.C. believes that any Englishmen will go to Australia to play under such an insulting menace they are optimists as well as ignorant of the game which they profess to control. The best toast anyone can drink to Australian cricket is: "Good health to an entirely new Board of Control."

A memorable and personal tribute from Jardine to Larwood.
The ash tray (very appropriate!) was presented before a crowd of
20,000 in England.

In 1950, Harold and Lois Larwood and family emigrated to Australia, arriving in Sydney on the SS Orontes - the same ship that took Jardine's team to Australia in 1932. From left: Cyril Roper with his fiance June Larwood, Enid, Harold holding Sylvia, Mary, and Lois Larwood holding Freda. They lived in Kingsford. Harold died in 1995 and Lois in 2001. Sadly June died in 2017 and Enid in 2019.

www.ingramcontent.com/pod-product-compliance
Lightning Source LLC
Chambersburg PA
CBHW030941090426
42737CB00007B/500